HOME THEATER
DESIGN

HOME THEATER DESIGN

Planning and Decorating Media-Savvy Interiors

Krissy Rushing

GLOUCESTER MASSACHUSETTS

QUARRY BOOKS

First published in the United States of America by
Quarry Books, a member of
Quayside Publishing Group
33 Commercial Street
Gloucester, Massachusetts 01930-5089
Telephone: (978) 282-9590
Fax: (978) 283-2742
www.rockpub.com

Library of Congress Cataloging-in-Publication data available

ISBN-13: 978-1-59253-308-4
ISBN-10: 1-59253-308-6

10 9 8 7 6 5 4 3 2 1

Cover image: Benny Chan/Fotoworks
Back cover images: Courtesy of Atlanta Home Theater (top);
                   Courtesy of Onkyo USA Corporation (middle);
                   Theo Kalomirakis (bottom)

Printed in China

To Ronnie, Richard,
Carrie, Riki, Rocky,
and John

CONTENTS

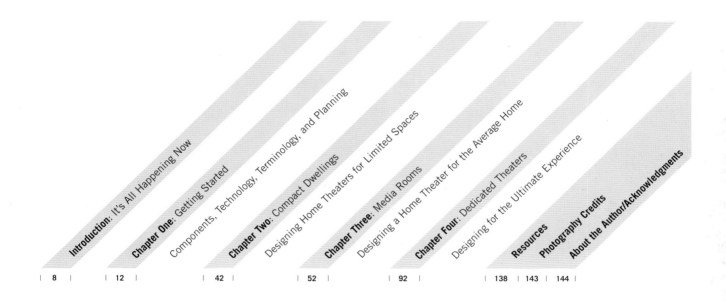

it's all happening now

Today's designers and homeowners face a new, generally unexplored challenge: designing a room with a media, or audio-video, element. Media rooms and home theaters are fast becoming as relevant to the home as kitchens, living rooms, and bedrooms. In fact, given the amount of time and money the average person spends enjoying television and movies, the home theater or media room now seems like a natural extension of the home itself—a room that was not feasible only a few short years ago.

The question is: Why is this happening now?

< Home theater is becoming as commonplace as the microwave or refrigerator. This book will help you learn how to incorporate one into your home.

∧ This MartinLogan speaker system features electrostatic floorstanding and wall-mounted models.

Imagine trying to construct an entire room around a 24-inch (61 cm) black-and-white TV that receives only three channels, all riddled with static, and that is encased in gaudy faux-wood cabinetry with an unsightly antenna poking up from its back. Or envision spending big bucks on a widescreen TV or speaker system only to watch jumpy, wobbling video and listen to muffled sound. It seems a ridiculous waste of time and money, doesn't it? But until relatively recently, these conditions were the harsh reality of the home entertainment arena.

The digital era has led us to another echelon of home entertainment. The invention and subsequent wild success of the digital versatile disc, commonly known as the DVD, has forged the way to this improved state of affairs like a scythe cutting through heavy brush. Though DVD is not the first video technology people have watched and enjoyed in their homes, it is the only format that has come close to mimicking the conditions of a bona fide movie theater in such a handy package. Laserdisc was promising but cumbersome, with a large, flat case like an LP record. Also like a record, it often had to be flipped over to get to the ending. Now DVD makes VHS tapes played on a VCR, with their tracking problems and poor video and sound quality, seem like relics. In the same way the compact disc (CD) ousted tape, the DVD has usurped the throne of videotape, and we are all the better for it.

Not only are DVDs more compact and more convenient than videos, the picture quality surpasses any video format to date, and only promises to get better with high-definition DVD on the horizon. DVDs also can be encoded with the same surround-sound format you appreciate at the movie theater to yield the same immersive surround-sound audio experience in the home. And, in addition to its spectacular audio-video quality, the DVD offers programming—such as special documentaries about the making of a film, behind-the-scenes footage, and commentary from the film's director—that you can't get anywhere else. DVD producers continue to push the envelope of creative ways to entertain people at home, adding value to their products, competing with one another, and ultimately making the medium an art form in its own right.

But what does any of this have to do with designing a room in your home? The answer is simple. The leaping advances in video and audio quality have dictated the wide-spread adoption of the home theater equipment that powers the DVD. To enjoy the sparkling video quality of a DVD, people are willing to invest in a widescreen television set or projection system. To listen to the DVD's surround-sound tracks, people are willing to purchase surround-sound speaker systems—whether affordable bookshelf speakers or a complete high-end floorstanding system. To run and power those speakers, of course, they need receivers, amps, processors, and so on. And with the investment made in the equipment, it makes sense to invest in the room itself, designing it to optimize the theater-at-home experience and to make the venue beautiful and comfortable. Home theater enthusiasts have become addicted to perfecting both their systems and the integration of those systems into a room. These theaterphiles are constantly upgrading their equipment and searching for the best software to play on it.

Although home theater is not an inexpensive hobby, creating a satisfying theater experience in your home will eventually have you scoffing at the thought of going to see a movie. The investment will help pay for itself in saved money on concessions, parking and movie tickets—not to mention save you the emotional turmoil of venturing into an overcrowded theater where you are subjected to advertisements and excitable adolescents pointing laser beams on the screen or laughing when they should be crying or vice versa. By committing to an audio-video system that is well integrated into a room, you regain the power to enjoy a safe, happy, comfortable movie theater that is completely controlled by your whim.

Home theaters and media rooms are also fast becoming a focal point for families to gather for quality entertainment and time together. Whether family members are listening to the new Fleetwood Mac DVD-Audio disc as background music in the kitchen, rooting for their team in the Super Bowl in HDTV on the living room big screen, or watching *Gone with the Wind* on DVD in the dedicated theater, the environment must be comfortable, which dictates a change in the way audio-video rooms are designed. We've all heard the term "toys for boys." Notoriously, in fact, the home theater has been an XY-chromosomed obsession, and, stereotypically, men aren't always the most design-conscious people in the house—that role has traditionally gone to women. As families integrate technical equipment into the decor of a room, and as that equipment becomes more approachable, women are also becoming more involved in the design of the home theaters and media rooms that now occupy space in their proud homes, often taking an active role in the creation of both the room and the audio-video system.

And it's all happening now. Consumers want home theater systems and rooms in which they and their families can enjoy them. The precedent for home entertainment has been set, and there is no turning back. Successful interior designers and homeowners who want to create one of these revolutionary rooms will embrace their technological future and adapt accordingly. This book will help you learn how to plan a media room or home theater and to anticipate the challenges involved in doing so. It will help you blend technology and elegant design—what some would consider an oxymoron—with skill and grace. You may encounter three tiers of home theater as you proceed. These, all based on lifestyle, budget, and spacial considerations, are discussed in this book.

The first chapter focuses on integrating an audio-video system into a small room, such as a townhouse living room or a den in a condominium. These setups are often simply home theater systems placed in the room rather than built into its structure or design.

Dedicated to multipurpose media rooms, the second section of the book focuses on rooms designed in a slightly larger, more flexible space, like you might find in a house. Media rooms generally serve more than one purpose, such as theater and living area, and work well when the audio-video equipment is folded into the design of the room so as not to be obtrusive when not in use. Media rooms have their own special considerations for maximizing the home theater system in the constraints of a functional living space.

The third chapter is devoted to the dedicated home theater, the ideal place in which to experience complete suspension of disbelief. This is the room that all audio-video buffs dream of owning, a place where the imagination can run wild and viewing conditions can be optimized.

This book is not for the tech nerd with the setup tool in his shirt pocket, if you'll pardon the typecast. Nor is it for those concerned only with the aesthetic principles and integrity of their room. Rather, it is for people, and their number is growing, looking to strike a happy balance between technology and decor—for people who want their rooms to be both beautiful and technologically state-of-the-art. If you are in this group, then this book is your guide to designing and integrating media-savvy interiors into your home.

Of course, you can take ideas from any area of the book and scale them up or down to fit your room's considerations, such as size and style. In fact, this book is best used as a guide rather than a map. Remember that on any memorable trip, half the fun is getting there. Venture off the main road and explore on your own. Find that charming hole-in-the-wall with great food and good wine no one else knows about. Many people in the audio-video industry have different opinions about the best route to your destination, and, therefore, there is no right or wrong set of directions, only opinions and guidelines. So grab your bowl of home-popped popcorn with real melted butter from your own fridge, a Coke or martini, and your remote control. Then sit back, relax, and enjoy the ride...and the show.

getting started: components, technology, terminology, and planning

Understanding the nuts and bolts

what is home theater?

A home theater system can be complex or simple. A simple system consists of, at the least, a video display, four speakers, a subwoofer, one or two sources, and a receiver. The Onkyo system shown here is straightforward, with the front left and right and center speakers hanging on the wall around the plasma display and the receiver resting on the table below, next to the subwoofer. Only one rear speaker is shown.

The jumpy 24-inch (61 cm) television you had in college, connected to a hand-me-down VCR and speakers circa 1980, hardly constitutes a home theater, at least not in any respectable sense of the term. A home theater is more than just audio and video slapped together like two pieces of bread to make a sandwich; it is the synergy of its components and the experience of the system within a comfortable environment. After all, they don't call it a system for nothing. Just like the body doesn't function without the heart or the brain, without all of the necessary moving parts of a home theater the system won't work, or won't work to its full potential. Your entertainment system can be as simple as a set of bookshelf speakers, a receiver, a DVD player, and a television along a wall of

your living area, as complex as a million-dollar dedicated theater with red velvet curtains and a projector nestled in your basement, or anything in between.

We present three levels of home theater integration in this book—small systems in small rooms, multipurpose media rooms, and full-on, dedicated home theaters. For each level, you can learn how to blend interior design elements with high-tech gear. First, however, it is important to know what all theaters have in common—namely, the electronic equipment that generates the experience—so you can understand all the moving parts before you begin to ponder the whole.

the nuts and bolts of a home theater system

All home theater systems and rooms have in common some bare-bones basic components. Although you do have quite a bit of choice in your equipment purchases based on budget, lifestyle, and personal taste, the nuts and bolts of all systems are similar. Therefore, this book does not address the nitty-gritty technical details of every wire, black box, and accessory but, rather, focuses on the components of a basic home theater system and how they relate to one another. The goal is to enable you to plan the space in your room, select furniture to house your gear, and help you incorporate the gear into the design of your room. In the end, when the lights go down, all of these parts make up a systemic whole that takes you out of your reality and into the realm of entertainment.

picture-perfect: the video display

The question of which is more important, audio or video, is hotly debated among home theater aficionados. Some desire the sound of a powerful explosion coming at them in surround sound; others appreciate the crispness and color accuracy of properly calibrated video images. Either way, one thing is certain: The video screen plays an extremely important role in the overall entertainment experience. After all, where would theater be without the act of viewing something, whether a live Shakespearean troupe performing *Romeo and Juliet* or a *Lord of the Rings* DVD projecting on a video screen. When choosing a video display, consider what size and type are best for your needs. This chapter focuses on size and proportion. The types of displays available are explained in greater detail in the following chapters.

size matters

Despite the recent trend of downsizing gear in the home theater marketplace—with the proliferation of bookshelf or "lifestyle" speakers and emaciated components—bigger is usually better when it comes to video. That isn't to say you can't find video screens, such as plasmas, with a small footprint and slim profile, but the surface area of the screen should be reasonably expansive. Screens, whether television screens or screens used with projectors (also known as projection screens), are measured diagonally. This diagonal measurement is a mystery to most consumers, who often have trouble translating diagonal length into a concept of screen size. The diagonal measurement stems from the era of excess, the 1980s. Marketing gurus saw an opportunity to make more money when they realized the biggest linear dimension of a rectangle is its diagonal measurement; advertising using this measurement made screens seem bigger and more virile to the public.

Choose as big a screen as you can, keeping in mind both the proportions of your living space and optimal viewing distances. (For more on viewing distances, see page 60.) The owner of a size-challenged New York loft, for example, might prefer a 40-inch (102 cm) television to a 120-inch (305 cm) projection screen, but the owner of an antebellum mansion with an airy spare room will welcome the larger screen.

When you're pondering television and screen sizes, keep these points in mind: Normally, televisions larger than 60 inches (152 cm) have their own built-in stand (their weight hinders them from resting safely on separate TV stands), are hard to move, and take up lots of space. Some people build custom cabinetry around floorstanding models to minimize their cumbersome appearance.

If your budget or room conditions prohibit creative cabinetry to hide the bulk of your big screen, rest assured that the benefits of the bigger screen, which allows for a more immersive experience and greater suspension of disbelief, outweigh the drawbacks. It's well worth the sacrifice.

Most sets smaller than 60 inches (152 cm) can be placed on a TV rack or other furniture that is strong enough to support its weight. Choose furniture to match the style of your room. For example, pick a sleek wire rack with frosted glass if your room is contemporary or minimalist in style; go for wood A/V furniture for a warmer, rustic look; or pick out funky, bright pieces to liven up a room.

> Choose a video screen that will fit comfortably with your lifestyle and room size. This small, modern loft incorporates a 36-inch (91 cm) direct-view television and medium-size speakers into custom cabinetry, conserving valuable wall and floor space.

< This chic floor-to-ceiling
cabinetry creation by designer
Ed Davis hides the unsightly
TV stand of a 60-inch
(152 cm) rear-projection
television. It also houses the
front and center speakers,
whose custom finishes blend
in with the curly maple wood.
Components are housed
behind cabinet doors. Theater
design by Bliss Enterprises.

< If your room is small, wall-
hanging speakers can help save
floor space. These wallhanging
Artcoustic speakers, which look
like art, add to rather than
detract from the room s
modern design.

sound advice: what you need
to know about speakers

Imagine sitting on the edge of a river. In front of you is the
sound of the river crashing around rocks; behind you, the sound
of feet on damp earth as someone approaches. Above, the
sound of birds chirping filters through the trees.

We live in a three-dimensional world, but reproducing its three-
dimensional soundfield in the two-dimensional world of movies
is not easy. That is why, for a truly permeating experience, a
basic audio setup consists of no fewer than five speakers, plus a
subwoofer (a 5.1 system), arranged quasisymmetrically around
the audience to re-create all the little hums, swishes, hisses,
and pitter-patters we take for granted every day in our three-
dimensional world.

Two front speakers, usually designated as front left and right,
or main, speakers, are positioned on either side of the screen.
The center speaker is placed logically above or even behind
(in the case of some projection systems) the video display.
(Some people put the center speaker below the screen,
but this isn't the best placement in terms of sound accuracy.)
This horizontal speaker, made to sit on top of a television set,
reproduces the majority of dialog from soundtracks.
Because sound travels more slowly than light, the center speaker
must be near the screen so the actors don't appear to be

lip-syncing. In other words, if the light from the screen
reaches your eyes before the sound from the speaker reaches
your ears, the actors will seem to be talking more slowly than
their mouths are moving.

Two rear surround speakers—dubbed the left and right surr-
ounds, or rears—are placed on either side of the seating area.
These speakers handle ambient noise and music and are often
quite active on dynamic soundtracks with myriad surround
effects, such as an explosion or a thunderstorm. The subwoofer
is positioned to the left or right of the television; it handles
low-frequency pressure (or bass) in a room. The sub gives your
theater the sensory response that makes the walls shake and
your chair rumble.

Discrete sound from a soundtrack, unique to each speaker,
is channeled, or distributed, to the five speakers and the
subwoofer, so you'll often hear industry buffs referring to 5.1
channels of audio when referring to a 5.1 surround speaker
system. Channels, simply, are the surround-sound information
going to the speaker, not the speaker itself. It is a slight
distinction, but one that can save you a headache as you
learn more.

> Speakers don't have to be eyesores in an otherwise blemish-free room. In fact, many speakers come in various finishes, such as cherrywood and glossy black, so you can incorporate them easily into the design of your room. Here, the light wood Infinity speakers are as much a design statement as the hardwood floors and big, airy windows.

< Just because your TV set is large doesn't mean it has to stick out like a sore thumb. This SIM2 rear-projection television is surprisingly svelte, and the red accents on its back are picked up elsewhere in the room.

design tip

video rule of thumb

Projection systems—a separate projector and screen—often require precise placement at a fixed distance from the video screen and tend to be expensive. This makes them good options for a dedicated home theater, which offers more placement options than a multipurpose room. Rear-projection televisions, which are 36 inches (91 cm) and up, are good for big media rooms, and direct-view televisions, which tend to be 36 inches (91 cm) and under, are ideal for smaller rooms.

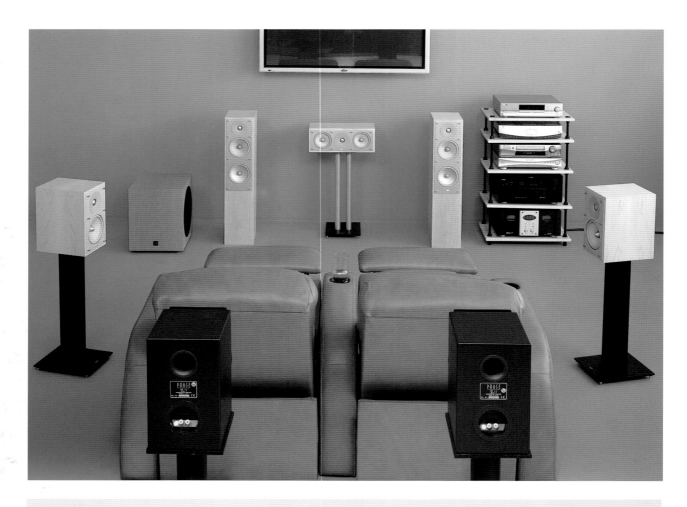

design tip

don't box me in!

Don't put speakers in corners. The sound will bounce off the walls, ceiling, and floor, producing reverberation and sonic reflections. Your main speakers should be several feet from the corners of the room.

Also avoid putting speakers (even so-called bookshelf or small speakers, much less freestanding speakers) in cabinets. Like a corner,

the enclosure of the cabinet can negatively affect the speaker's sound. Instead, use speaker stands, or mount small speakers on walls.

Of course, every rule has exceptions. Some people like the boomy quality of the bass they get when they place their subwoofer in the corner, so this rule doesn't necessarily apply to these low-frequency connoisseurs.

Custom cabinetry is another exception. Acoustical engineers and cabinet makers often take the back baffle, or enclosure, off the speaker and allow the box shape of the cabinet to act as the speaker's rear enclosure. They tweak the sound of the newly boxed-in speakers with an equalizer.

An even easier option is to use architectural, also known as inwall, speakers in a custom

cabinet. Architectural speakers don't have a back baffle and use the inside of the wall in which they are placed as their rear enclosure. Many architectural speakers can be painted or covered with acoustically transparent fabric, so you can match them to the color of your cabinetry.

< Basic Home Theater Setup: This photo shows how a basic home theater should ideally be set up. For a 5.1 surround sound system, you'll have five speakers, plus a subwoofer. For a 6.1 or 7.1 system, an additional speaker or speakers are placed directly behind the audience.

v This medium-size room, which moonlights as a music haven, incorporates a 40 inch (102 cm) floorstanding video monitor and Infinity tower speakers that fill the space with sound. The center speaker sits on top of the display for attachment to the video image.

design tip

central location

Put the center speaker as close to the video image as possible. Make sure it is magnetically shielded so it doesn't interfere with the picture or damage any VHS tapes in the vicinty. Don't use your TV's speaker as a center channel or use mismatched speakers (especially for the front left and right and center speakers). Buying speakers as a sonically matched set ensures they have the same capabilities and sonic characteristics, which, in turn, will give you smooth, even sound.

The Scoop on 6.1 and 7.1

If you are among the many who believe that more is better, five speakers plus a subwoofer may not do the trick. They didn't for George Lucas, who was the first to encode a soundtrack—for *Star Wars: Episode I—The Phantom Menace*—with a sixth-rear center surround-sound channel for its theatrical release, causing theaters all over the globe to fit their screening rooms with a sixth rear-center speaker. Speakers arranged in the typical 5.1 setup, either at home or at the cineplex, do not provide sound behind the viewer's head, such as, in the case of *The Phantom Menace*, Naboo starfighters traveling from the rear, behind audience members, over their heads and onto the screen in front of them. With this new rear center channel, you can literally hear the starfighters coming from behind you before you see them.

Lucas's engineers made this work by taking soundtrack encoding going to the two rear surround channels and filtering audio data from both into a sixth matrixed rear channel. Matrixed simply means that the sound going to the sixth channel is not discrete—that is, engineers do not give this channel its own unique information but derive it from other channels. A receiver or processor simply manipulates the soundtrack to create a phantom rear-center channel. Naturally, once this technology premiered in theaters and went on to be included in *The Phantom Menace* DVD, consumers simply had to have 6.1 technology in their homes. Getting 6.1 at home requires a rear-center speaker, a 6.1 processor or receiver to translate the 6.1 soundtrack scheme, and a DVD with a 6.1 soundtrack. Of course, you can still listen to 6.1 discs on a 5.1 system, but the information that would normally be matrixed to the rear-center channel will stay, most likely, in your rear left and right surround speakers.

If one rear-center speaker is just not enough, a 7.1 system might be just the thing for you. A 7.1 system has two rear-center speakers that usually both play the same thing. (You'll need a pre-pro or receiver that is 7.1 capable.) Why do you need two speakers behind you pumping out the same noises? Simply put, some people think two speakers sound better than one—that the dual rear centers spread the sound behind a viewer's head, making the soundfield even less choppy from speaker to speaker. Receivers that have 9.1-channel capability have recently been introduced—that's nine speakers plus a subwoofer.

Whether or not you utilize 6.1, 7.1, or even 9.1 technology is entirely up to you. Some people like the extra speaker or two behind them to complete the drafty hole in the 360-degree soundfield. Others either don't want to spend money on extra speakers or a new receiver for the added benefit or don't have the space to put these extra speakers. Demo a 6.1, 7.1, or 9.1 system to decide if it is right for you. If you are upgrading from a 5.1 system to a 6.1 or 7.1 system, make sure to buy a rear-center speaker(s) that is identical to the speakers you already own. If you are starting from scratch, look for manufacturers that sell complete 6.1 and 7.1 speaker packages.

may the source be with you
getting your entertainment

Sources are the soul of home theater. Without them we would have nothing to watch, nothing to listen to, nothing to keep us entertained. DVD players, VCRs, laserdisc players, CD players, digital video recorders, satellite television, and even cable television all pump the stuff we want to see and hear into our systems. That's why picking sources is largely left to personal preference. Tailor your sources to your own desires. If music is not important to you, focus on video. You can, for example, use your DVD player as a CD player, eliminating the need to buy a separate CD transport.

On the other hand, if music is your main interest, put more time and money into perfecting your system's audio portion. In this case, you might spend your money on a 500-disc CD jukebox or a Super-Audio CD/DVD-Audio (SACD/DVD-Audio) universal player to play your collection of high-resolution audio on rather than a costly projector and high-end DVD player that would just collect dust. Focus on those areas of your entertainment system that are going to make you happiest.

Money Matters: planning your room budget

As for any home improvement project, having a budget is crucial before you begin building a home theater or media room. The first step is to determine the kind of room you want to build. Do you want to spend all your money on the system and none on the room itself? Do you want to spend a little money to integrate your system into your room, perhaps installing custom cabinetry or motorized lifts to hide your TV or projection screen when it's not in use? Or do you want to go all out, spending big bucks on a complete dedicated theater, renovating the room from head to toe, and installing theater chairs, a stage, the works? Based on how much work you want to do and how much of it is doable according to your wallet, determine your overall budget.

Once you nail down your budget, figure out your priorities for the room. Is video more important than audio, or vice versa? Make a list of all the things you might want to spend money on, then decide what percentage of your budget should be devoted to each of them. Of course, you need a little leeway to buy things you forget to list, such as that last-minute component video cable or speaker wire. The following sample budget shows how to plan a small system. Use it as a basis for whatever kind of room you are going to create, whether similar in scale to this one, a media room, or a dedicated home theater.

This home theater system came in $710 under budget. It might be a good idea, in this case, to consider where to reallocate those funds. A 36-inch (91 cm) television seems a little small for a system with a $2,000 receiver and a $2,000 speaker system. The extra $710 may allow this theater's owners to jump up to the next size model. If not, the extra money can be put toward future upgrades.

To scale this budget to your room, consider the particular needs of the space. For example, you might want to build a custom lift for your plasma display, allowing it to rise out of the floor when you are ready to watch television. Budget for this cost. For a dedicated theater, allocate more for a video projection system, theater furniture, or help, such as a wiring expert or specialist to accurately calibrate your video display.

But regardless of your plan, make sure to have at least a rough idea of what you are going to be spending before you begin so you can shop without either going overboard or skimping. You will thank yourself later when you have the perfect system for your needs and when your credit card bill comes in the mail.

design tip

shopping with smarts

Do your research. Both print and online sources abound that provide information, even reviews, of home theater equipment. Just as you would spend time researching a car you'd want to buy, take time to research components for your home theater. After all, you are making a big investment in an important room of your home.

If you have no idea where to start when it comes to selecting equipment for your room, puchase one of the many home theater buyer's guides available on newsstands. These guides provide the manufacturer, model number, features, and price of thousands of products on the marketplace. (One particularly reliable source is the *Home Theater Buyer's Guide*, published annually.) Once you find a product that seems to match your requirements, search for in-depth reviews by industry professionals both in print and online. These reviews can act as guides to determine how well the product performs.

Remember, however, that the way a speaker performs is more subjective than the performance of a properly calibrated video display. Also keep in mind that video displays are usually precalibrated in stores to look good under the store's conditions. When you get your television set home, you'll realize that what looked good in the store may not look good in your home. You can, however, always hire a certified technician to come to your house and calibrate your video display.

ITEM	PERCENTAGE OF BUDGET ALLOCATED	MAXIMUM AMOUNT TO SPEND	ACTUAL COST	MONEY SAVED IN BUDGET
VIDEO				
36-Inch (91 cm) Direct-View Television	15	$1,500	$1,100	$400
SOURCES				
DVD Player	8	$800	$649	$151
SACD Player	5	$500	$425	$75
D-VHS VCR	10	$1,000	$1,049	−$49
AUDIO				
Speaker System	20	$2,000	$2,199	−$199
PROCESSING & AMPLIFICATION				
5.1 Receiver	20	$2,000	$2,235	−$235
CONTROL SYSTEM				
Touch Screen Control System	5	$500	$499	$1
SOFTWARE				
New DVDs	2	$200	$185	$15
ACCESSORIES				
Speaker Cable	3	$300	$234	$66
Wires	2	$200	$90	$110
Miscellaneous	5	$500	$275	$225
ACOUSTICS				
Diffusers, Bass Traps	5	$500	$350	$150
TOTAL	100	$10,000	$9,290	$710

< Receivers incorporate the
functions of both an amplifier
and a processor. This one,
by Rotel, also has a
DVD–audio/video player.

> If you have a bit more room
in you budget, you might
consider getting "separates"—
a separate amp and processor.
If you do, make sure to allot
space in your rack for
these components.

receivers: the brains of your system

Imagine you're running with the bulls in Spain. You hear the
low grumbling of their hoofs on the pavement, you see the first
bull's horn round a corner, and you run like you've never run
before. Why? Because vital information gathered from your
sensory organs was relayed to your brain, which, in turn, relayed
a message to your legs to get moving. Similarly, without a
central processing unit to gather and decipher information,
your home theater's legs won't hit the pavement. A receiver
acts as the brain in your home theater. It comes with a gaggle of
inputs and outputs on its rear panel that lets you connect your
speakers, your sources, your video display, and allows them to
communicate with one another. A receiver also decodes
soundtracks from surround-sound-formatted source material,
such as a DVD's Dolby Digital 5.1 soundtrack. Then it takes
surround effects and delivers them to the appropriate channel,
or speaker. A receiver provides power, measured in watts, to
every speaker in your system. Switching is also handled by this
jack-of-all-trades. Switching allows you to change from one
source to another, such as a DVD player to satellite television,
without having to shuffle plugs into your TV, which can
accept no more than one or two sources at a time.

When shopping for a receiver, seek one that has the
surround-sound decoding capabilities you require. That is,
if you plan to listen to 5.1 home theater, make sure your
receiver is Dolby Digital- and DTS-capable. Also, be sure the
receiver has all the inputs and outputs you need. For example,
if your TV has a component video output, buy a receiver with
a component video input. Most midpriced receivers have
one of everything (although the phono input for turntables
is becoming increasingly rare), but it pays to double check.
Receiver manufacturers also throw in a dizzying array of digital
signal processing (DSP) modes to make you think you are
getting more bang for your buck. With a DSP mode, you can
make your room sound like everything from a church, to a
hall, to a stadium, which begs the question: Why would you
want your home theater to sound like any of these venues?
Take DSP modes with a grain of salt.

amps and processors versus receivers

If multitasking isn't your thing, you know that to get jobs done right, you have to do them one at a time. A receiver does everything from processing surround sound to powering speakers to switching between sources. However, if you have a bit of money to spare, you might want to consider buying a separate amplifier and surround-sound processor. An amplifier's sole responsibility is to provide power to your speakers. Because it is dedicated to this task, it usually provides cleaner power, and more of it, than a receiver can.

Meanwhile, a receiver's surround-sound processing duties can also be done by a separate surround-sound processor (sometimes called a preamp/processor or pre/pro). With a separate amp and processor, these two duties are done individually—in different stages, in different chassis—so the audio signal stays pristine.

Receivers are fine for small home theaters and lower-budgeted media rooms with fewer sources and small speakers that don't require heavy loads of power, but separate amps and processors are well worth considering for dedicated theaters with more sources and bigger speakers that require more power.

When you are planning your theater, it is important to decide early between separates or a receiver so you can plan your space and system accordingly. Amps, for example, are outrageously heavy, so you have to purchase a rack that can accommodate the heft of the unit. They can also be quite expensive, so it is good to budget for them from the beginning.

accessorising

Just like any good wardrobe is enhanced by the perfect belt or bag, a home theater system can be improved with a variety of accessories. Equalizers, for example, fine-tune and maximize the sound in your room once you've installed your speakers. If a dinosaur is walking onscreen, tactile transducers (also referred to as buttshakers), located under the seats or the floor will make your body shake with each step of the prehistoric beast. Video accessories, such as line conditioners and scalers augment picture quality, while power enhancers clean, condition, and regulate the power coming from your electrical outlets and going to your components. The list of accessories keeps growing. Talk to a salesperson at your local A/V shop, consult a home theater enthusiast magazine, or do research online for more information on accessories and how they can make your outfit look and sound like a million bucks.

everything you ever wanted to know about surround sound but were afraid to ask

The list of acronyms used for surround-sound formats is positively confusing. The following list of soundtrack formats will help you shop for DVDs, receivers, and surround-sound processors.

Dolby Digital

Also known as AC3, this encoding system is usually found on DVD-video and DVD-Audio discs. Most receivers and preamp/processors are capable of decoding Dolby Digital. Its big advantage is that it digitally compresses up to 5.1 discrete channels of audio into a single bitstream, which makes it fit on DVDs and HDTV broadcasts (you'll need a Dolby Digital-capable digital satellite receiver for HDTV, of course), where other, uncompressed surround-sound formats simply won't fit.

Dolby EX

An enhancement to Dolby Digital, Dolby EX (often referred to as 6.1) adds a rear-center channel to 5.1 soundtracks. The sixth channel is matrixed from the left and right surround channels. You can listen to EX soundtracks on a 5.1 system, (EX is, in industry lingo, backward compatible with 5.1) but to obtain the benefit of the added rear channel, you need a 6.1 processor and rear-center speaker.

DTS

DTS, which stands for digital theater systems, is a digital sound-recording format that premiered in theaters with the film *Jurassic Park* in 1993. DTS, which is less compressed than its competitor, Dolby Digital, necessarily takes up more room on a DVD or live broadcast. To some, however, this less compressed format sounds better than Dolby Digital. This often leaves DVD producers wondering if they should sacrifice other information on a DVD, such as bonus materials, for the improved sound quality of DTS. Most receivers and processors are DTS-capable.

DTS ES

This 6.1-channel surround format, like Dolby's EX, creates a sixth channel from a 5.1-channel soundtrack. When the soundtrack is denoted as DTS ES Discrete, the sixth channel has been engineered to be unique, not matrixed, which simply means that original audio information was created specifically for the rear-channel speaker, not derived from other channels. To take advantage of these soundtracks, you will need a processor or receiver with DTS ES decoding capabilities and a rear-center speaker. While many receivers

and preamps have this feature, DTS ES DVDs are sometimes hard to find.

Dolby Pro Logic

This format derives a left, center, right, and mono surround channel from two-channel Dolby Surround-encoded material via matrix techniques.

Dolby Pro Logic II

Pro Logic II is an upgraded version of Pro Logic, which improves decoding for two-channel soundtracks and music.

Dolby Pro Logic IIx

Dolby Pro Logic IIx technology provides home theatre enthusiasts with a solution for 7.1-channel playback of traditional stereo and 5.1-channel content by extending the matrix decoding techniques first introduced in Dolby Pro Logic II and Dolby Digital EX. The technology, incorporated into a receiver or processor, will provide home theater enthusiasts with a flexible upgrade path, allowing them to connect extra channels and speakers to their 5.1- or 6.1-channel systems. It is also the first technology to offer the choice of processing traditional stereo music and movie content into a 6.1- or 7.1-channel listening experience.

Mono

Monophonic sound is found on films made before the advent of stereo and surround sound. Mono sound is often divided between the front two speakers or presented from the center speaker.

DVD-Audio

DVD-Audio is an enhanced audio format with up to six channels of high-resolution 24-bit/96 kHz audio encoded via the Pulse Code Modulation (PCM) compression scheme onto a DVD. To enjoy DVD-Audio discs you need a DVD player. DVD-Audio discs will not play on SACD players or traditional CD players, but you can purchase a universal player to enjoy both high-resolution music formats.

SACD

Super-audio CD, owned by Sony, is an enhanced audio format with up to six channels of high-resolution audio encoded using the direct stream digital (DSD) compression scheme. To play SACD, you may need an SACD player. However, most SACDs, such as Pink Floyd's *Dark Side of the Moon*, are hybrid discs that can be played on CD players as well.

< This equipment rack s hidden behind a red art deco triangular proscenium that surrounds the screen. When the rack must be accessed, the art deco cabinetry slides over to expose the gear.

the rack

Television and gear racks can be tricky. Before you purchase one, you should have some idea of what you are looking for. First and foremost, you need to know the size or the weight of your television. For example, some racks are specifically designed to hold 36-inch (91 cm) TVs, while others can handle units up to 50 inches (127 cm). Most racks are specified for the size of TV they can hold, but some list weight capacity only. It is a good idea to measure the dimensions, especially the depth, of your TV to make sure it will not hang off the edges of the rack; some TVs are bigger than others.

The next points to consider are the number of components you will need to house and whether or not the shelving in the rack will accommodate them. If you have a DVD player, a CD carousel, a VCR, a satellite receiver, a receiver, and a laserdisc player, you need a rack that will hold all six components. Again, it is a good idea to measure each component. A CD carousel that houses CDs vertically instead of horizontally might not fit in the rack you've chosen; then

you'd be stuck putting the carousel on the floor or elsewhere, which is bad home theater karma. Some racks, however, have adjustable shelving, giving you a bit more flexibility. Because A/V furniture is designed for technological equipment, it can get very complex. You can't just pick out a pretty piece of furniture and expect everything to be hunky-dory when it's time to install your system.

Racks have intricate wire-management systems that allow you to run your wires discreetly through the furniture so the audience can't see them. Many racks are made of special materials that reduce vibration from your speakers and provide a stable plat-form for your system. The idea is to isolate each component so it can do its job unfettered by rumblings from your subwoofer and the like. The legs of some racks are hollow tubes you can fill with sand or other materials to absorb vibration. Most racks also have spiked feet, also common with speaker stands, that keep your rack from moving around and help isolate it, and your equipment, from the floor.

If you are going to use glass shelving, make sure the glass is thick enough to support your gear. Amps, in particular, can be quite heavy; sometimes they exceed 150 pounds. Another nice touch is matching your speaker stands to your rack. Many rack manufacturers offer matching racks and speaker stands in materials from sleek steel to inviting wood.

Be wary of the upgradeability of your system when purchasing a rack. If you plan to add other components as your system matures, make sure to purchase a rack with more shelves than you presently need. As an alternative, consider that many manufacturers offer modular racks you can purchase and add to your existing rack.

Any rack you purchase should have holes for wires in the rear, if it is enclosed, and a ventilation system. Gear pumping power to your system can get hot. A lot of racks are open so plenty of air can get to the components. After the investment is made, the last thing you want to do is come home to a rack full of melted gear.

There is also a variety of wall-mounted gear racks that can be quite stylish. If you decide to wall-mount your gear however, be careful when putting heavy components on wall mounts, especially if you don't want to caulk and repair walls should you ever move.

Whatever you decide, shop around and don't skimp on your gear rack. It is going to be with you a long time and will go a long way toward integrating the entertainment system within the room as a whole.

< The industrial look of this two-channel listening room comes from the exposed racks of gear—the focal point of the room.

ʌ There is a variety of manufacturers that specialize in audio-video furniture, so virtually any look can be created in your home. This steel furniture by Boltz will house a basic home theater system, with two shelves for components, and one for a display.

< A small bar in this San Francisco media room doubles as an equipment rack and media storage facility. (More views of this room are featured on 136 and 137.)

> The gear rack in this dedicated home theater is obviously one of the room's main attractions, with a place for the homeowners' record collection.

wire management

running wire to speakers

Getting from point A to point B can be a challenge in the world of home theater. Sure, running wire to the speakers next to your TV is not a problem, but if you want to reap the benefits of surround sound, you are going to have to address those floorstanding surround speakers next to the seating area and the wires they require. How are you going to get wires across the living space from your receiver or amp to the surround speakers without tripping over them or feeling like you are traversing a snake-infested jungle?

Solution 1: Creative Carpeting

Run speaker wires under the carpet. A custom installer can do this for you, or you can do it yourself. The process is usually as easy as moving furniture, lifting the carpet, running the wire, then laying the carpet back and securing it in place. Of course, if you have hardwood floors, this isn't an option. If you're looking for a quick fix, an area rug may cover wires as well as give your room better acoustics. Inevitably, however, snippets of wire will show where the area rug doesn't cover the entire floor.

Solution 2: Overhead Wiring

Some folks run wiring from the wall behind the main gear rack up to the ceiling and around its perimeter, then down the wall where the back speakers are located. Most speaker stands have wire-management systems that allow you to run wire through the stand and into the speaker with discretion. Another option is to install crown molding over the speaker wire. The drawback of this approach is that if something goes wrong with the wiring, it is difficult to move the molding and replace the wires. Installing the crown molding also can be tricky because you need to avoid putting nails through the wires. Recently, some manufacturers have introduced faux crown molding that you can run wires through and then open and close the molding as needed. The molding can also be painted to match your decor.

Solution 3: Baseboard Wiring

Run wires around the baseboard of the room. Go up and around doors, of course, and never across a door's entryway. You can also use wire covers, which are little strips of plastic or rubber that hold the wire firmly in place; they are available at any hardware store. Wire covers also blend into the wall and can be painted, making the wiring almost invisible.

Solution 4: Going Wireless

Some manufacturers offer wireless speakers. However, this technology is relatively new and, without power pumping directly into a speaker, it probably won't have much sonic impact on the main home theater or media room. Wireless speakers might be acceptable for a small bedroom or secondary system.

the subwoofer problem

There are two types of subwoofers: passive subwoofers, which derive their power from other speakers, the amp, or the receiver and, therefore, require no power outlet; and powered subwoofers, which need their own power supply. If you have a powered subwoofer—you guessed it—you need a power outlet located near the subwoofer. This is one reason you often see subwoofers near the front of the room and off to the side a bit. Attaching a subwoofer to a wall outlet and a speaker wire often makes placement difficult unless you use an extension cord—and generally, the fewer extension cords, the better.

component wiring

Wires behind your TV and receiver can also get out of hand, often looking like piles of mutated spaghetti crawling out of gear and pooling on the floor behind the TV stand. Many commercial wire-management systems are nothing more than glorified trash-bag ties or clips. Whatever system you decide to use, make sure your wires are organized and untangled. It sometimes helps to label wires so when you are disconnecting or connecting them you know which is which without having to follow each one back to the receiver.

> If you are installing custom cabinetry, like that shown here, or are buying a piece of audio-video furniture, make sure there are holes in the back so wires can escape.

compact dwellings: designing home theaters for limited spaces

Creating an optimum experience in smaller rooms

> This small room hosts a home theater system that doesn't detract from the fireplace, which is the focal point of the room. The home theater is neatly tucked in a cabinet next to the fireplace; a center channel is above the television, a small subwoofer is below the screen, and two surround speakers are mounted on the walls. System design by Future Home. Interior design by Thomas Biggert Design.

"Design in art is a recognition of the relation between various things, various elements in the creative flux." —D. H. LAWRENCE

Though many of us dream of sprawling mansions with hundreds of rooms, we aren't all there yet. Some of us are happily ensconced in our own cozy cabins or bungalows, in lofts in densely populated cities where space is at a premium, or in townhomes and condominiums. And, yes, some of us even rent apartments. If you have a small space, naturally your home theater options are going to be proportionally limited. Your choices for equipment will be fewer, as you will need gear compact enough to allow the room to serve other purposes as well. In other words, a small room with a home theater system is just that, and not necessarily a home theater room.

In fact, trying to force a big system into a small space can be hazardous to your health; like eating a whole chocolate cake by yourself, the big system just won't fit. If you are one of the many whose 800-square-foot (74.3 square meter) apartment will not tolerate a 60-inch (152 cm) widescreen and speakers with a 10-inch (25 cm) footprint, however, you still have options. In fact, some wonderful systems were designed with you in mind. Whether you are on a tight budget or not, you can find small systems for every room type. First, however, you need to find a space in your place for your system. Then it's time to go shopping.

where do I put my system in my small room?

You've downsized your apartment, have already parted with your king-size bed in favor of a queen, and have even turned in your armoire for a simple dresser. Now you're expected to find more room for a home theater system?

You may be tempted to cram everything in a corner or against a window, but before you do, check out the following guidelines, which will help you properly place your system in your room.

< A compact living/media room is equipped with a 60-inch (152 cm) television fitted into custom cabinetry by Jay Meepos of Concepts by J. By putting the television within the wall, the floor is left free for other purposes, such as relaxing in this uncramped room with a film or sitting by the fireplace.

> An innovative bookshelf by designer Noor Adabachi of Spiral III Designs includes a functional ladder for reaching books and an enclosure for the two-channel music system.

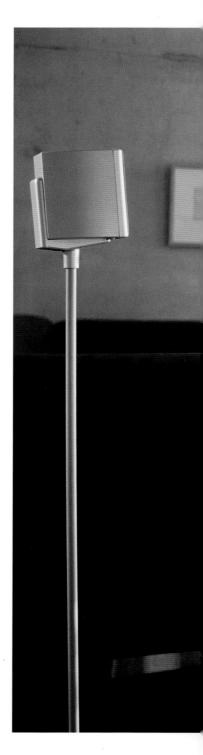

> While placing your equipment in the corner, as here, may save space, if you don't position your seating area at the same slant, you may experience eye and neck strain. System by Canton.

draw a floor plan

Drawing a floor plan of your small room will help you find the best place for the system. Make a rough diagram of your room as it exists, noting windows, electrical outlets, doors, and closets. Ideally, you don't want to put the TV on the wall opposite a window, as you will encounter a lot of glare during daytime viewing. Of course, you could cover the windows with blackout drapes, but this isn't necessarily the best look for your apartment's living room. Do the best with what you have.

corner placement: a pain in the neck

If your longest horizontal wall is only 16 feet (4.9 meters) and you buy a 60-inch (152 cm) TV that's 4.5 feet (1.4 meters) wide, speakers that are a foot (0.3 meter) wide each, and a subwoofer that's 2 feet (0.6 meter), you are already taking up more than half the wall with equipment, not counting the space you need to leave between your television set and your speakers. If you're working around a door or window, the situation is even worse.

Some people choose to angle their display from the corner into the room instead of flush against a wall, but they then often make the mistake of placing the seating parallel to a wall. Unless you place the couch or seating at the same angle as your television set, you are going to be taking a few trips to the chiropractor. Of course, the problem with putting your couch at the same angle as your TV in a small room is that half the room will be inefficiently used, eating up space and making the room feel cramped, cluttered, and very un-feng-shui.

It is infinitely better to choose more compact equipment that will actually fit along one wall of your room. Instead of the 60-inch (152 cm) TV, for example, choose a 40-inch (102 cm) TV and smaller speakers. In fact, with a large set in a small room, you run the risk of not being able to sit far enough away from the screen. After all, mother was right: sitting too close to the screen can hurt your eyes.

Edit yourself when buying a home theater system and remember, you can always buy mammoth speakers when you move into a bigger place. One beauty of home theater is that you can upgrade.

> A home-theater-in-a-box, like the one shown here by Onkyo, is a logical solution for a small room or for people just entering the world of home theater. The components are easy to hook up, inexpensive, and compact.

check your wiring

Another danger of putting large gear in a small room is power handling. If you are trying to plug an amp, processor, DVD player, television, and CD player into your room's single electrical outlet, you run the risk of shorting your equipment—and, if you're renting, who knows if the wiring is up to code? Surge protectors, an accessory you can buy at your local A/V store, will help guard against this. You can also buy power enhancers, which condition the electricity powering your system, helping prevent shorts and uneven power handling.

home-theater-in-a-box

What though the field be lost, not all is lost for the small dwelling. All-in-one solutions are available inexpensively and are virtually painless to install. A home-theater-in-a-box (HTiB) should contain five speakers, a subwoofer, and a DVD unit that also acts as a receiver, handling surround-sound decoding and sometimes amplification duties, plus all the necessary cables to get you started. All you have to do is add the television.

The units are usually compact, with small, identical speakers and a subwoofer, not to mention one black box instead of four or five, saving you valuable real estate. They often come with sleek

speaker stands or wall mounts. The speakers are so small, however, you can most likely stand them next to your TV or on side tables around the seating area. Because they can't provide enough power and amplification to fill bigger rooms, HTiBs, in fact, are ideal for small rooms. In general, they don't compare with the impact of separate components and speakers, but they are a good place to start for those new to home theater.

HTiBs are easy to set up, often featuring color-coded wiring that lets you know which wire goes where without even reading the directions. Most HTiBs decode Dolby Digital 5.1, and some decode DTS 5.1.

design file

hallway home theater

Dedicated home theaters don't have to be in the biggest room in the house. A bachelor in Newport Beach, California, created a home theater in the lower level of his beach house by transforming a hallway into a haven. The space was big for a hallway but had four entrances that had to be concealed. The first was a sliding glass door that led to a patio. A custom cabinetry carpenter was called in to design an equipment rack in front of the door, giving the homeowner access to the back panels of the gear from outside the house. A second door, leading to the garage, was covered with a faux fabric wall containing acoustic insulation material that helped tame acoustic reflections. The third entrance, a stairwell from the upper level of the home, was fitted with a sliding door on sensors that opens and closes when guests enter the home theater. The fourth entrance, the door to a guest bedroom, was covered with fabric to match the walls, and a lever to open the door was recessed in the wall. This example shows that even the smallest homes can be fitted with home theaters by making efficient use of space.

> A listening room is a place to enjoy music. This room features rear acoustic diffusers and one chair placed directly in the sweet spot, where the listener gets the best sound.

a two-track mind:
listening rooms for the stereo-inclined

As many theater designers will attest, it is difficult to create a room that is equally adept at reproducing music and movies. Different sonic capabilities are needed to reproduce, say, a bomb exploding in *Saving Private Ryan* than to do justice to the Vienna Philharmonic's rendition of Wagner's *Der Ring des Nibelungen*. Usually there are tradeoffs. But before there was surround sound, there was stereo—two speakers delivering audio to your ears. In the world of consumer electronics, there are devout stereophiles who prefer analog to digital, two speakers to five, and music to movies. If you are one of them, you don't have to be left out in the cold when it comes to building a room dedicated to your hobby. Listening rooms are highly engineered havens where you can meditate on your two-channel music in an environment dedicated to this purpose.

The first thing to do is select your equipment. You'll need two identical speakers, a preamp plus an amplifier (or a two-channel receiver), and a couple of sources. When choosing your sources, consider the kind of music you will be enjoying. Do you like the high resolution of Super-Audio CDs? Then you'll need an SACD player (most SACDs are hybrid discs, meaning they will also play on a CD player, but not to their full potential). DVD-Audio music can be played on any DVD player. If you like both DVD-Audio and SACD, go for a universal player that will accept both formats as well as play CDs. (Remember, also, that with the advent of DVD-Audio and surround-sound music, you can enjoy a wide variety of music releases on your surround system.) If vinyl is your thing, purchase a record player, but make sure your other gear, be it a receiver or a preamp, has a phonograph input. Stereophiles often use tube amps, which are separate amps for each channel or speaker, instead of an amplifier with all channels in one chassis. Some stereo speakers are specifically designed for two-channel, not 5.1-channel, use.

In a home theater, the center channel above the screen anchors the sonic image to the video screen, so audience members who aren't directly in the sweet spot (off axis) can enjoy a precise soundstage. In a stereo setup, however, sitting off-axis dramatically affects the soundstage. It is important to sit in the sweet spot in a listening room. That is why listening rooms often contain only one chair, in front of and directly between the two speakers.

assessing the room

As we saw in chapter two, being restricted to one room, such as a condominium's main living space, limits choices. Only a narrow list of alternatives is available, such as all-in-one home theater solutions versus individual components. With a large home, presumably with multiple larger spaces that can serve as a home theater, you are presented with a range of exciting and often daunting decisions.

The first determination you'll make, which seems obvious but is often taken for granted, is which room will make the best theater. If you have a choice of two rooms of roughly the same size, choosing a space based on aesthetics (for example, a magnificent marble fireplace in the foyer) may not be best if the room has a less favorable floor plan.

Because more options require better planning, it is wise to assess your rooms before making a final decision. In doing so, take into account your lifestyle, the desired style of the room, and the room's floor plan.

lifestyle considerations

Lifestyle, needs, and priorities translate directly into requirements for your media room; a truly balanced room cannot be designed without considering such personal requirements. If you frequently entertain guests, for example, you probably want the theater room to serve double duty as a place for socializing—where people can gather, eat, and drink prior to watching a film. Whole-house audio is a good option for frequent party-throwers; it allows background music to waft through multiple rooms and onto the patio via speakers throughout the home. If children are going to use the system, it must be simple to use, perhaps with parental locks, and the room's furniture should be durable. A gear junkie, on the other hand, will concentrate on high-end exposed equipment rather than chenille throws or color-coordinated accent pillows.

Take into account your room's special needs. Do you want to put a pool table at the back of the room? Perhaps you want the room to include a bar or dining area. These room attributes must be determined at the beginning of the planning process, not tacked on as an afterthought. For example, retrofitting a room with a bar or kitchenette, or rethinking structural factors such as windows, electrical outlets, and cabinetry, is not as easy as creating space for such features in the first place and planning accordingly.

Also consider what your priorities are for the media system itself. If your primary interest is supplying background music, your emphasis should be on installing a great sound system. If you want to use the room primarily for watching films, focus your efforts on a state-of-the-art video display. Whatever your particular lifestyle, room needs, and priorities are, make sure to give them serious consideration at the design phase of your room.

< New York designer Glenn Gissler designed this home theater to have a simple, minimilast feel but to also be inviting and comfortable for the homeowners.

> A touch-panel control screen rests in a central location, controlling everything from house security to air-conditioning, drapes, lighting, and audio-video.

the automated home of the future

You're having a party that starts at five o'clock—just before sunset. Imagine hitting a button on your touch-panel control system that reads "Party, Dusk" and instantly, every light in the home goes to a predetermined level ideal for that time of day. The drapes open or close so the view is just so, outdoor architectural lighting is turned on, and music from your preselected party CDs queues up at just the right volume, playing throughout the house, from the atrium to the dining room to the pool area. As the sun sets, the lights automatically

go up to make up for the loss of natural light. Later, your guests decide to use the karaoke machine, and a camera positioned over the stage relays the video to various plasma screens throughout your home, allowing people on the patio to watch their friends butcher respectable tunes inside. All the while, you aren't worrying about a thing. In fact, you're enjoying a martini with your guests instead of playing the overtaxed host or hostess. Such are the benefits of whole-house audio and video and a good control system.

You can take advantage of this "smart home" technology in your own house by installing a multiroom system and a control system. A multiroom system delivers sound and video to more than one zone of your home. The first zone is your main system, where the DVD player, CD player, amplifier, receiver, and main video display are located. Whatever is being played in this first zone can be broadcast throughout the home's other zones. If your wife is watching a Marilyn Monroe movie in the kitchen, you can watch it from the comfort of your bedroom. Many receivers

and surround-sound processors offer multiroom/multizone capability, and some even offer the ability to play different sources in each different zone. For example, if you're having an *I Love Lucy* DVD marathon in the home theater, your daughter can listen to music while doing her homework in the study.

The control system is the quarterback of a multiroom system. This approach to home theater, however, can get highly technical and expensive. Such systems often require the help of an outside custom installer.

creating a room style

gear integration

The style of your media room is one area where you can really express your personality and interests. Style doesn't apply just to furnishings and color schemes but also to the gear you choose and how you present it. Some people like to show off their gear or make it a design element of the room. Manufacturers understand how gear integrates with a space and design their equipment with this in mind; they try to create elegant, stylish, sleek equipment that won't be a blot on the landscape. Freestanding speakers have become quite lovely, acting almost like miniature sculptures or monoliths in a room. Likewise, gear racks can be exposed to give the room an industrial, technical feel. Your poker buddies will be impressed at the wall of steel and blinking lights in your home theater.

Other people prefer to keep gear completely hidden when it isn't being used so they can enjoy the room without that very same wall of steel and blinking lights glaring at them. When it's time to watch a movie, the video screen lowers from the ceiling, a projector rises from a customized coffee table, and motorized shades emerge from the wall to cover the windows. Electronics are kept in a special closet, and architectural speakers are hidden in the walls. Whether you choose to expose or conceal your system, the decision enables you to allocate space properly within the room.

∧
> This media room in Malibu serves as a bright sitting area—but when the blackout shades drop, the screen falls from the ceiling, and the projector is exposed, it's showtime. Custom cabinetry hides all the equipment when it is not in use.

> If you must have bright colors on your home theater or media room walls, make sure they are cooler hues as in this blue room, and not pinks, reds, or pastels. Overly colorful walls will affect the color rendition of your video display.

< Because light colors reflect light and interfere with the projected image, it is important to choose dark, muted colors for your home theater or media room, like the deep purple tones of this theater.

design tip

theater in tote
Go to a hardware store and select color chips that match your patterns or color scheme. Carry them with you—you never know when you are going to come upon a vintage movie poster at a garage sale or piece of artwork at an auction that will work fabulously in your home theater. When you do encounter these treasures you'll need to know if they are compatible with your colors.

picking a color scheme

With luck, you did not set your heart on canary yellow, eggshell white, or powder blue for the main color of you room. A cardinal rule of home theater is to make the room as dark as possible without causing eyestrain. Lighter-colored walls tend to reflect light back into the room. Instead, choose a deep color such as burgundy, purple, dark blue, dark green, dark gray, dark red, or black for the walls and the main furniture, using lighter colors for accents, such as pillows—a sort of photonegative of the traditional living room. Similarly, smooth textures reflect light while rough textures absorb it, so avoid glossy paints and mirrors; stick with matte finishes, textured walls, and fabrics.

If you already have furniture, work with its colors and textures to plan the color scheme for the rest of the room. If you simply cannot live without your red velvet loveseat, design your color palette around it, incorporating new furniture seamlessly with the old. Likewise, if you have an existing set of speakers, use these as a starting point around which to build the rest of your home theater system.

media storage

Whether your room has ample closet space or none at all, you are going to have to find a place to store your collection of music and videos. You can choose to expose it to the world, keep it hidden, display it artfully, or use a jukebox. Whatever you choose, make sure media storage is convenient, organized, and safe, and that it coincides with the room's style.

The Library Look

Are you particularly proud of your extensive collection of DVDs and want everyone to see it? Open media storage might be the choice for you. Racks that let you show off and organize DVDs and CDs make a statement—much like books in a library. The colorful spines and slim profiles can be a source of pride. Wall shelving, freestanding bookshelves, and doorless cabinetry are all options for showing off your collection.

Out of Sight

If the last thing you want to do in your living/media room is look at a bookcase full of DVDs, laserdiscs, and CDs, then concealed storage is a must. Cabinets with doors or closets might be the way to go. You can use existing cabinets or closets for storing your DVDs and CDs—sometimes it's just a matter of installing shelves in a closet or clearing out a cabinet to make room for your media.

If you don't have closets or cabinets, a cabinetmaker can install cabinets or drawers that are built to order and blend with your decor. Many furniture makers also provide media storage units or entertainment center furniture that includes media drawers.

Storing with Style

Many handsome media storage racks are available. Sleek racks, modern shelving, wire bookcase-style racks, colorful plastic containers, and wooden cases are just a few of your options. Pick a style and color that suits your room and needs. Think outside the box as well; creative solutions are often the best. For example, if you have a narrow but tall section of wall that would be ideal for storing your media, have a furniture maker build cabinetry and install a ladder, giving a unique twist to an otherwise bland bookshelf.

Jukeboxes and DVD Carousels

Much like traditional jukeboxes, CD jukeboxes and DVD carousels allow you to store and play your discs in the same place. DVD and CD carousels or changers can house up to 700 discs and eliminate the need to load and store your DVDs. The units allow you to enter specific title information for your music and videos and store it electronically. When you are ready to watch a DVD, simply call up the title using the remote control and press Play. If you run out of room in one jukebox or carousel, most units let you daisy chain (connect) another jukebox to increase your storage capacity. This option isn't the most glamorous one if you want to show off your collection, but it certainly is convenient.

Storage Do's and Don'ts

Believe it or not, DVDs, CDs, laserdiscs, and VHS tapes can be damaged if improperly stored. Keep media out of direct sunlight to prevent warping, and store it in a cool, dry place. If you have DVDs and CDs, store them so the disc itself is vertical; horizontal storage can cause them to lose their rigidity. In general, discs, such as CDs and DVDs, are a little sturdier than VHS tapes, which can degrade over time.

> You can get as fancy or as understated with your media storage as you like. Oftentimes, you can find media storage furniture, like the IKEA furniture shown here, at any furniture store.

< If you have plenty of room and
a big enough budget (or simply
a lot of laserdiscs and DVDs
to store), you can build an
entire subroom in your theater
or media room specifically
devoted to housing equipment
and media, like a library.

planning your audio and video

Once you have selected the room based on the various considerations discussed above, it's time to make your audio-video plan. The assumption here is that a media room's goal is to create the best theatrical experience possible in a dual-purpose room. This entails understanding how sound and video work within a room. Don't fret. Nobody is asking you to calibrate a television or measure speakers for flawless sound. That's an engineer's job. But designing a home theater demands that you at least have an idea of the technical matters engineers will consider so you avoid planning an unworkable room or one that will intrinsically deliver subpar audio-video.

We'll start with the audio plan, as it involves the entire room layout. Sound issues are dictated or created by the room itself—from the place you set your couch, to the skylight above it. From a design standpoint, a video system is less complicated; planning it can be as simple as choosing a television.

< This sophisticated room eschews the traditional theater look, opting for comfortable chairs and ottomans, but maintains the theater feel with the big screen, which is enclosed in custom cabinetry when inactive.

audio design

selecting size-appropriate equipment

Albert Einstein discovered that an object in motion remains in motion unless acted upon by an outside force. This rule of physics holds true for sound coming from your speakers. Ultimately, it is harder for sound to fill a larger room; the sound will just keep moving into the atmosphere until a wall stops it. Therefore, a 20- by 40-foot (6.1 meter by 12.2 meter) room will allow the sound from the speakers to bounce off the walls and back to the viewer, keeping it contained and powerful. On the other hand, in a 40- by 60-foot (12.2 meter by 18.3 meter) living area with cathedral ceilings, sound can get lost.

For your speakers to fill the void, they need to be mighty (or at least more capable than the typical out-of-the-box solution). While vast advances are being made in small bookshelf speakers, a good rule of thumb is the bigger the speaker, the more powerful it will be. It's simple: A small room can have small speakers; a medium-size room, medium-size speakers; and a big room, big speakers. With that rule established, here are a few ways to maximize the sound in your living room.

Look at the power rating of your speakers and amplifier (if you have one) to determine if they are going to do the job with ease or strain to make a sonic impact. If you have a receiver, now is a good time to upgrade to a separate amp and surround-sound processor. Receivers are wonderful solutions for small rooms and tight budgets, but they can't drive speakers quite as well as an amplifier, which is specifically designed for the job.

However, the system's speakers must be able to handle that power. In other words, you don't want to hook up bookshelf speakers to a high-powered amplifier; the amp will fry them with an influx of power.

making a large room sonically manageable

There are tricks to making small speakers sound larger than life in a big room if, for some reason, bigger speakers are not an option. If the room is spacious, for example, don't place your furniture against the wall opposite the theater system and expect to get good sound. The speakers won't have enough power to reach the audience. Instead, place the couch closer to the video screen and front speakers, as if the room were smaller, allowing the sound to reach the listeners without losing steam.

Another option is to strategically place furniture to create surfaces for sound to bounce off of, thus containing it even in a big room. A wooden armoire, a Chinese screen, or a bookshelf can help concentrate sound around you rather than allowing it to disperse into the vastness of the room. Some acousticians may disagree, but in a home media room, tweaking acoustics isn't as important as it is in a dedicated theater, where sound can be controlled with greater accuracy.

< Vaulted ceilings look good but can wreak havoc on the acoustics of the room. Before you install a home theater system in a room with poor acoustical conditions, consider all the other rooms to which you could add a media element, then decide which will work best for you.

design tip

audition your speakers

Always audition speakers before buying them, keeping in mind the space you are working with. Manufacturers and audio-video stores will be happy to accommodate your speaker tests. Also keep in mind that speakers sound different after they are broken in over a period of days; the speakers become less rigid and their true sonic character comes to the forefront. It is good to make sure the store where you purchase your speakers has a return policy, in case you don't like the speakers' sound after they've been broken in. Some retail outlets break-in speakers before they sell them to you, so you know exactly what you are buying.

> Architectural speakers are good options if you want your speakers concealed. Here, the speaker is painted to match the pattern on the ceiling.

< If you have a large room with vaulted ceilings, sound can get lost among the rafters. One solution is to make sure your speakers are large enough to fill the void. Bookshelf speakers won't do the trick.

the pros and cons of architectural speakers

When a room has plenty of wall space, it makes sense to consider architectural, or inwall, speakers. Architectural speakers are a popular choice for media rooms that serve additional purposes, such as casual music listening, and for kitchens, dining rooms, bathrooms, and living areas. These speakers offer both great sound and aesthetic appeal. Freestanding speakers tend to visually dominate rooms, which may not be a problem for the audiophile of the house but might bother someone who uses the room for socializing or relaxing with a book. (Of course, you can also use freestanding speakers to make a statement.) Inwall speakers reduce clutter, are available in many designs and styles, and can be installed in the ceiling or walls. Because they mount flush with the wall, they take up little space and draw less attention to themselves. Some speakers can even be painted or covered with acoustically transparent fabric to match the color of your walls.

Architectural speakers do, in most cases, mean tradeoffs. First and most obvious, they require that you cut holes in your wall. Unless you are willing do a lot of drilling and patching, you are stuck with the position of your speakers once the hole is cut—and you won't know how the speaker is going to sound in the wall until you put it there. This prohibits you from experimenting with the sound and sound response of the room by moving the speakers around and trying different placement. Some inwall speakers address this problem by allowing you to pivot the tweeter to face different directions, allowing for some positioning flexibility after installation. Another problem in a larger room is that inwalls may be far apart or too far away from the sitting area. Yet another issue is that a speaker's enclosure plays a key role in its performance. Inwall speakers don't have a back enclosure; they use the wall itself as the back enclosure, which

makes the sound more unpredictable. And architectural speakers
can cause vibrations of the walls themselves, anything inside
the walls, and anything hanging on the walls. Inwalls also break
a room's shell, potentially allowing sound to leak between the
theater and other areas of the house.

The benefits of concealed speakers are fast coming to outweigh
their drawbacks, with manufacturers improving their sound
and making them easier to install. If possible, listen to several
models before buying and give your placement serious thought
before you start knocking out drywall.

∧ Can you see the speaker in this
room? It sits in the wall on the
left, completely camouflaged.

rules of thumb for architectural speaker installation

In the Music-Intensive Home
The location of speakers whose primary purpose is to provide background music can be driven by aesthetics. However, try to mount the speakers at ear level—it is better to hear sound coming directly from the speaker rather than bouncing off walls and furniture. Place speakers symmetrically, if possible.

In the Home Theater
Speakers should be aligned horizontally through the middle of the video image. In other words, don't install them in the ceiling or at ground level. Follow the Basic Home Theater Setup arrangement on page 24. If you can't get your speakers as close as you want to the viewing area, simply do the best you can.

taming room rattle

You've no doubt seen the famous Maxell ad with the fellow sitting in his chair, holding on to the armrest for dear life, his hair blown back, facing his sound system. As anyone who has stood next to a large speaker at a concert can attest, sound can move you, both physically and emotionally (indeed, a busted eardrum can make you weep). A loud blast from the subwoofer can cause all sorts of vibrations in your media room. The good ones you feel in your body; the bad ones you hear coming from air-conditioning ducts or the chandelier. Make sure everything in your room, from the pipes in the walls to light fixtures to paintings on the walls, is securely in place. While this is not necessarily a problem in a smaller room, where the speakers and sub-woofer are less powerful, if you have a large room with large speakers, you may encounter problems.

Experiment with the volume levels of your theater to determine at what point the art on the walls starts to shake or the room starts to clatter. If the rattle and hum bothers you, take steps to correct it. This can be as easy as sticking double-sided tape underneath the picture frames or as complicated as opening sheetrock to tie down pipes. Where the theater is being built from the ground up, test the home theater system before the drywall goes up, which will allow you to make changes before the room is finished.

> This speaker is hidden in a cabinet equipped with an accoustically transparent cover. The cabinet also houses the of the home-owner's CD collection.

∧ Some speakers are designed to look like artwork. The Artcoustic speaker shown here can be customized with your own design.

> Plasma displays are fabulous choices for rooms where you don't have a lot of floor space. Many manufacturers make matching speakers that hang on the wall next to a plasma, such as the B&W speakers shown here.

creating a video plan

Making the image on a video display look good can be complicated, involving calibration and lots of tweaking. However, making the video display look good in your room is a cinch—it's as simple as choosing a TV and deciding how to present it. (Projectors, also a good option for video displays, are a little more complicated.)

Today, there are more types of televisions than ever. Plasma displays, direct-view TVs, rear-projection TVs, and high-definition capability are all options to consider. Luckily, styles have changed since the days of antennas and those ungodly monstrosities encased in tacky wood you'll find in some octogenarians' abodes. Because the shape, style, and function of a TV can vary depending on the type, shop in terms of your room's specific design needs, then take into account your technical inclinations.

plasma displays

Thin is in, and the plasma TV is the svelte sister in a family of fatties. Because of its lightweight, slim chassis, plasmas are easy to place in your room. You can hang them on the wall or place them on top of a mantle without feeling that nagging desire to hide them like a blemish. They are aesthetically pleasing and easy to incorporate into a living room or feature as a focal point of a dedicated theater.

The plasma video quality, however, has a few shortcomings. While plasmas are bright, they have trouble turning off the light, so blacks can look dark gray instead of truly black. False contouring, another problem, is when the picture looks a bit uneven. However, as advancements continue to be made, these difficulties are being resolved. Among their pluses, plasmas, unlike rear-projection sets, offer a broad viewing area, meaning audience members sitting on the sides of the plasma (also known as sitting off axis) will get just as bright and crisp an image as those sitting front and center. However, plasmas are among the priciest TVs, so they may not be an option for everyone. Rest assured, however, that prices are coming down as plasmas become more mainstream.

creating a bedroom home theater

The bedroom is a place of rest and relaxation. That is why bringing technology into this sacred, intimate space can often be jarring. But there are ways to gently incorporate a media element into your bedroom without upsetting its quiet atmosphere.

To plan an audio-video system in your bedroom, start by determining where you will be sitting. The first place that comes to mind, naturally, is the bed. A bed is, indeed, a cozy place to snuggle up and watch a late-night romance or thriller, but to make the experience truly comfortable, you will want to follow some simple guidelines.

First, consider the height of your bed. Do you have a four-poster bed that requires a stool to climb into? Do you have a futon that is low to the floor? The height of your bed will determine where you put your video screen. If you have to look down from your four-poster at the screen, you are going to get uncomfortable. Likewise, if you strain to look up at your screen from your futon, you'll be constantly moving to get a better viewing angle.

Start by sitting upright against the headboard of your bed or against pillows on the wall if you don't have a headboard. Settle in and get comfortable, propping yourself on pillows if that is what you'd normally do when watching television from the bed. Look at the wall ahead of you where you might put your video screen. Are your sightlines clear? For example, some beds have footboards that block the sightline if you put the video screen directly ahead of you. If so, adjust the position of your screen accordingly. If you have a footboard, you might put the screen slightly higher on the wall so you don't have to prop yourself up to see all of it.

Also, consider your feet, which, if you are lying down, may intrude on your sightline. If so, again, raise the screen slightly. Television sets that must be placed on a TV stand or dresser, however, may pose problems if the surface is not high enough. The same goes for floorstanding models—it is neither feasible nor attractive to put phone books under a TV. That's why plasmas are good choices for the bedroom; they can be placed on the wall, as high or as low as you want them. You could even put a separate video projection screen and projector in your room.

< White cabinetry that matches the bed in this room makes the room uniform and relaxing.

> This airy space features a small plasma. The plasma is discreet, allowing the view outside to be the main focal point of the room.

∧ > This bedroom by designer Holger Schubert features a plasma display on a rotating pole. This allows the audience to enjoy it from either the sitting area or the bed. Red curtains evoke the spirit of a movie theater in the bedroom.

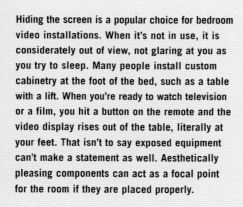

Hiding the screen is a popular choice for bedroom video installations. When it's not in use, it is considerately out of view, not glaring at you as you try to sleep. Many people install custom cabinetry at the foot of the bed, such as a table with a lift. When you're ready to watch television or a film, you hit a button on the remote and the video display rises out of the table, literally at your feet. That isn't to say exposed equipment can't make a statement as well. Aesthetically pleasing components can act as a focal point for the room if they are placed properly.

Some people find it hard to go from watching a movie in bed to sleeping in the same bed, finding the transition from the stimulus of entertainment to unconsciousness difficult. Consider putting a small sofa in the bedroom in front of the video screen and reserving the bed for sleeping. Another solution is to watch with one or two small lights on (preferably placed to the rear of the video screen to prevent glare) rather than in complete darkness; then, at sleep time, change the room environment by turning off the lights.

A television monitor—a set without a tuner— makes a fitting video display for the bedroom. Because you can't get channels, this approach makes your bedroom a comfortable place to thoughtfully enjoy a film rather than a haven for couch potatoes mindlessly channel surfing.

And the bedroom certainly isn't an appropriate place to pump up the volume—you don't want to shut off the speakers only to find your ears ringing when it is time to go to sleep. Choose smaller speakers that unobtrusively blend with the decor of your room. Also, make sure your equipment is completely off before you start counting sheep. Noise from A/V equipment can be distracting.

> When the owners of this media room aren't using the theater, they allow the sun to come in, making the room more pleasant. When it's time to watch a movie, blackout drapes emerge from the ceiling to create ideal viewing conditions.

room problems and design challenges

Every room presents idiosyncrasies and design challenges, but you can minimize their negative effects and work around the obstacles. Certain problems won't bother you; others will be sticking points. Consider what it is going to take to fix a problem—taking into account time, budgetary, and construction constraints—and then decide whether the issue is that important to you, and if so, come up with creative ways to address it. Windows, awkward room dimensions, and difficult wiring situations are just a few design challenges rooms can pose, but every room is different. Some rooms are more amenable than others to becoming home theaters.

the unbearable lightness of light: windows in your home theater

For you to enjoy a film in all its cinematic glory without having to pop aspirin for eyestrain or a headache, the room must have little or no ambient light. While the bay window in the den presents a lovely view of the garden, it by no means enhances your view of the screen. Sunlight, and even moonlight, can compete with the light from the TV screen or projector, which—if the ambient light wins—can wash out the image you're watching, making blacks look gray and colors faded. If you're using a TV, uncontrolled light can also cause glare on your screen, so you have to strain your eyes to see it.

When the soundtrack to your new James Bond DVD starts mingling with conversations about lighting the barbecue taking place outside, you'll soon realize that windows allow sound as well as light to come in and out of a room, competing with the sound system and distracting viewers. Windows also allow sound to leak out of the room, disturbing inhabitants of adjacent rooms. A room with French doors off the kids' room or a room that looks onto the pool area where people sit and socialize is not as sonically ideal as an isolated study with a couple of windows facing the backyard. In fact, the more isolated the room is, the better.

Choose a room with few windows or windows that are easily covered, lessening the need for customized window treatments, or install motorized drapes. Windows are a fact of life, especially considering that, unless you have a very large home or estate, the media room is most likely also an office, library, or living room. In these cases, when the theater is not in use, natural light is an asset, not a liability. So don't build a brick wall in front of your window just yet; you have other, less drastic options.

window treatments

You can identify the neighborhood videophile by the foil or black garbage bags covering his window. Taming light is important for a good image. The following approaches can help you cover your windows without resorting to such tacky solutions.

Motorized Drapes

Some companies install motorized drapes that stay hidden when not in use. They can be tailored to your windows and connected to a control system. When it's time to watch a film, simply touch a button on your control system; the drapes drop, shutting out most ambient light, and you are ready to go. You can even program the control system so the drapes open or close at specified times, such as dusk. Most companies offer a spectrum of drape colors to match any decor. You can also buy individual motors for any drapes or blinds.

The Velvet Curtain

Did you ever notice that most theater curtains are made of thick, dark, heavy velvet? There is a rhyme and reason behind this cultural phenomena. Not only do thick curtains keep out light but also they can tame unruly room acoustics. If you have a room that is "bright"—that is, sound tends to bounce off the walls and flooring, giving the room a lively sonic character or perhaps an echo—heavy drapes and window treatments can muffle the sound rather than bouncing it back at the audience, balancing reflections and making the sound less blunt around the edges. The curtains not only absorb sound within the room but also stop it from leaking out into other rooms, meaning you don't have to hold back when you crank up the volume. Velvet is great for this purpose. It can be used to hide the screen as well as cover windows. Be careful, though; it's possible to put too much fabric in the room, making it acoustically dead—that is, too much sound is absorbed.

Acoustic Windows

If you want to take your interior design a step further and really get technical, you can order special acoustically sealed windows that will greatly reduce sound transmission into and out of your room. You can also get special doors that function in a similar way, sealing sound within the theater.

Picking the Right Colors

Stay away from light colors, such as whites, light grays, bright colors, and pastels, which can reflect light and detract from the video image. Opt for dark or medium hues and stay away from shiny fabrics, like satin, and diaphanous or translucent fabrics, which allow light into the room. Choose matte finishes and opaque window treatments instead.

Window Shades

Perhaps the walls in your room are covered in fabric and the floor is covered in carpet. Chances are you do not need any more acoustically damp material, or material that absorbs rather than reflects sound. In this case, window shades may be appropriate; they will give your room a needed kick, allowing sound to bounce off their hard surface and reflect back at the audience rather than fall dead on soft fabric. Shades or shutters can be automated to slide down from above or rise up from below the windows. They can be customized in various finishes, including wood and varnishes, to blend in seamlessly with the room. Miniblinds won't necessarily keep all the light out but can be purchased with remote controls for convenience.

How Far Will You Go?

Violating the traditional rules of interior design, some people have been known to patch up windows or put furniture in front of them. Unless the room is a dedicated home theater, covering windows is not recommended. The effect looks awkward from outside the home. Further, sunlight is excluded even when the room is not being used as a theater, making it feel cavernous and uninviting during the daytime.

sizing up awkward room size

If you've ever blown air over the top of a jug of water, you may have noticed the sound is different depending on how much water is in the jug. It also varies with the shape of the bottle itself because it bounces off the water and the sides of the bottle at different frequencies. Likewise, the way sound interacts with the shape of a room varies from case to case. A room with lofty ceilings and a lot of open space is going to sound quite different than a rectangular space with low ceilings.

Most home theater designers prefer a room's dimensions to be in odd numbers. For example, a 13- by 33-foot (4.0 by 10.1 meter) room is preferable to a 14- by 34-foot (4.3 by 10.4 meter) room because in rooms with even dimensions, what are known as standing waves develop that cancel out sounds. What happens is that sound waves traveling in one direction combine with sound waves bouncing back in the other direction. The result is that some areas receive intensified sound but sound waves in other areas cancel each other out, creating sonic "holes" in the room. The room's shape affects the incidence of standing waves. Avoid perfectly square rooms or rooms precisely twice as long as they are wide. In an ideal situation, waves are evenly distributed throughout the room. An equalizer can be used to fine-tune your room's sound if you have problems, or you can hire an acoustician to come and tune the room.

design file

bowling alley dimensions
What's wrong with a long and skinny media room? The dimensions will wreak havoc on the room's sound, creating odd frequencies or sound dropout. A room that is 42 feet (12.8 meters) long by 15 feet (4.6 meters) wide, for example, can be cut in half to improve the theater acoustics. You can make the extra space into a kitchenette with a wet bar, refrigerator, popcorn machine, and concession stand. Choose smaller seating for the theater to give audience members more breathing room from side to side.

design file

log cabin luxury
Even a log cabin can be equipped with a state-of-the-art theater. Normally you can knock holes in drywall to run wire or make room for architectural wall speakers. With a log cabin, however, holes must be carved out of the logs for every piece of equipment. Wiring, too, is extremely difficult, as one vertical hole cannot be drilled through the series of horizontal logs. Instead, wire is run horizontally through individual logs, which is time-consuming but protects the integrity of the structure.

design file

sliding glass doors
Suppose the only room you have available for a media room has a rarely used sliding glass door that offers a view of a dog run or fence. The door also makes the room both too bright and too noisy. Although this clearly violates the principles of Interior Design 101, for home theater purposes that sliding glass door can be transformed into a cabinet for a clunky rear-projection TV. The TV is placed in front of the sliding glass door and a cabinetmaker builds a cabinet around it, sealing both the TV and the door in a sort of box that shuts out light and sound. Conveniently, the sliding glass door gives users access to the back of the TV from outside the house.

wiring woes

Luckily, you are probably not going to personally execute your room's wiring. A custom installer or electrician can help with this process, which can be difficult and require considerable patience. Thus, when you choose your room, consider how hard it is going to be to wire. Your goal, in this respect, is to streamline time and money spent on wiring. In general, a room built from the ground up is a lot easier to wire because you can get inside the walls before they are enclosed. Retrofitting wires in existing walls can get messy. When you remodel an existing room, you must snake the wires from one point to another through a wall. Wiring for electricity, speakers, phone, and cable must be considered in every media room, especially those with inwall speakers. Some rooms, of course, are more difficult to wire than others. A room of solid concrete, such as a basement, is going to give you a hard time, perhaps requiring special concrete borers to drill holes for wire. If you are transforming a garage with only one electrical outlet into a home theater, you will most likely have to hire an electrician to equip the room with enough electricity to power all your electronics.

design file

a room with a view
A Seattle home's living room has large bay windows overlooking Lake Washington. The homeowners don't want to obstruct the view, but because of the way the furniture is arranged to take advantage of it, the video display must indeed go in front of it.

Instead of disfiguring the vista, a motorized lift holding a plasma display is installed in the floor, its top covered with the same taupe carpeting as the floor. When the home-owners are ready to watch television or a movie, the plasma screen pops out of the floor. When they aren't watching the plasma, it remains hidden, and the view of Lake Washington is intact.

home theater feng shui

- Just because your theater is full of electronic equipment doesn't mean it has to be devoid of life. If your theater has windows, hang flowering plants to help keep the air fresh and to add color.

- Clear away clutter. Avoid stacks of magazines and disorganized CDs and DVDs.

- Hide all wires. There is nothing worse than a home theater with exposed wiring. It gives a feeling of disorganization and looks messy.

- Put a small backlight behind your TV or screen area to prevent eyestrain in a completely dark room. Install a gooseneck lamp near your seating area so you can read the back of a DVD cover without having to get up to turn the lights on.

- When arranging furniture, remember that less is always more. Ensure enough room for everyone, but keep in mind that too much furniture can make you feel cramped, restrict the room's flow, or make the space feel smaller.

- Decorate the walls; blank walls can look stark. Add personal touches like favorite artwork, photographs, or tapestries. Placed strategically, these adornments can also help tweak room acoustics.

- The theater is a place of escape. Remove clocks and telephones to keep distractions to a minimum.

- Always dim the lights when enjoying your theater. Lights can be distracting, drawing your attention away from the screen to other items in the room, such as a magazine on the coffee table, and they also cause glare.

- Situate the theater near a bathroom for easy access, if possible.

- Remove appliances, such as a small refrigerator or coffeemaker, from the room; their background noise detracts from the theater's sound. Put appliances in a separate room or closet near the theater.

- If possible, avoid having the theater's door behind the audience; opt for doors on the sides of the theater.

dedicated theaters: designing for the ultimate experience

Creating a full-scale media experience

the luxury of a dedicated theater

We all like to dream, and it is no wonder that a dedicated home theater is the ultimate fantasy of audio-video enthusiasts. A dedicated theater is designed for the sole purpose of facilitating a completely immersive audio-video experience. Such a room becomes an oasis from the rest of the house, a place where you can get away from the troubles of the day and isolate yourself in a wall-to-wall, full-scale media experience. If done right, the experience can rival and even surpass a trip to your local cineplex. Unlike a small system placed in your condominium's living room or even a well-integrated media room that doubles as a recreation room, a dedicated theater gives you complete, unabashed control over the room's environment, allowing you to create ideal conditions and manipulate them at a whim. But the dream comes at a price. First of all, surrendering a room solely for media purposes is impractical for many. Further, building a dedicated space typically necessitates a substantial budget. But if these hurdles can be overcome, you can have a whole lot of fun.

"Technology is not an image of the world but a way of operating on reality." —OCTAVIO PAZ

get a plan, get a guide

If you assume that all you need to install a dedicated home theater is a spare room and a bonus check, think again. The road to A/V paradise is wrought with pitfalls and peril that can lead you into a financial quagmire. Therefore, just as any great adventurer embarking on a fulfilling journey should do, you must plan ahead and have an experienced guide. Planning means carefully considering and maximizing the options available to you. For example, rather than struggling with ambient light or noise from other parts of the house, think about trading rooms to pick the most isolated area. Keep in mind that a dedicated theater is used only to crank those massive speakers and enjoy your new projector with some popcorn and the *Matrix* trilogy on DVD (or *Driving Miss Daisy*, if that's your cup of tea). Therefore, why do you need pretty bay windows? Pick the room that nobody likes or visits—you know, the one that doesn't qualify as a living room, family room, den, or even a spare office. The point is to create a tomb in which the only light comes from the projector and the walls are soundproofed.

Planning throws open the door to creativity. While putting up movie posters of *Texas Chainsaw Massacre* in your dining room might make dinner guests lose their appetite, and one of *Finding Nemo* in the family room be construed as gauche or infantile, both images are perfectly appropriate for the dedicated home theater. To be blunt, because it is a theater, you can feel free to make it look like one. This obviously leads us to building out and designing a themed theater. There is a beautiful home theater in the Los Angeles area totally dedicated to James Bond; the owner of the home, a huge Bond fan, took full advantage of an opportunity to create his own fanciful space in which he honors all four of the Bonds. A homeowner in rural Virginia designed her dedicated theater to resemble the Nickelodeons she grew up with on the Jersey shore. Planning allows homeowners to pay tribute, reminisce, relax, and entertain, all at the same time.

<> Atlanta Home Theater took care of the technical side of this Tuscan retreat in a Southern California home, while Theo Kalomirakis masterminded the theater's interior design. When the screen isn't in use, a vista of a Tuscan village is displayed (far left).

In planning your theater, a guide can be incredibly helpful. Those of us who can't kick start the juices of imagination can call upon one of the well-regarded companies that specialize in creating intricate original and turnkey theme theaters. Two industry luminaries are Atlanta Home Theater and Theo Kalomirakis, who collaborated on the Tuscan village and skyline shown here, complete with twinkling skies above and a well-stocked wine cellar in the back. The theme of resurrecting a piece of Tuscany in a converted living room came from a simple discussion between the homeowners and designers about the best place they had visited during their many travels. Now, every time they go into their dedicated theater, they travel back to Tuscany to enjoy a nice bottle of wine and a good flick—no passports required.

A guide is important not just to help design a theme or conceptualize your approach but also to help you navigate the technical decisions involved. With a small-room theater, we did our best to maximize the A/V experience. Media rooms presented their own challenges but allowed us to create a solid theatrical environment in the midst of multipurpose functionality.

But a dedicated theater means more than working in flux and on the fly. It actually demands a degree of exactness if we're going to achieve the proverbial theatrical experience at home. Accordingly, unless you have the technical expertise to wire a room and determine the appropriate acoustics for your theater, it is best to hire a guide, sometimes called a custom installer, to work with you through this process. But you need not simply hand over the reins of your dream room design to a professional. It is important to keep yourself in the loop when working with a home theater team. The following discussions are intended to illuminate some of the misunderstood and seemingly complex aspects of home theater design, both technical and physical.

Keep in mind that the goal is to create an environment that will satisfy each of your key senses (sight, sound, touch) and bring you and your family years of enjoyment. So don't just hand the project off. Understand what is going on, and be a leader who walks with your guides rather than behind them. This will make your expedition a fulfilling one.

what is your style?

As we've learned, no room can be properly designed without examining the lifestyle of the people who are going to use it. A dedicated theater designed for a reclusive bachelor, for example, will have an entirely different dynamic than a theater designed for a family with six children. Eight viewers is a lot of people! This number will dictate the way seating and, in turn, the gear is arranged. Let's consider, too, that this family may want to offer seating for the friends who will presumably visit; this will decrease space in the room and allow fewer options in placing or arranging those seats.

Whatever your lifestyle is, you still have to consider how to arrange the theater, leading us to an age-old question:

which comes first? the chair or the audience?

Forget about the chicken and the egg and that other mindbender about angels dancing on pins. Dedicated theaters have their own cool and controversial dilemma: which comes first, the seating or the people? The question is difficult but the first one we must address when working out our floor plan. As discussed previously, this decision is one your guide can help resolve.

Let's talk about the crux of the issue. There are dozens, if not hundreds, of manufacturers that design and build beautiful and comfortable theater seats. We're talking top-quality stuff. Some custom installers believe you should select the seats that are going into your space first and only then decide how many people will fit in your theater. This approach makes a lot of sense if one of your criteria is comfort before accommodation. It would be the perfect way to plan for the bachelor, who can buy the biggest and most comfortable chair in the world with little regard for guests.

Of course, problems may arise at the large family's home if their installer selects the same world's-most-comfortable chair but can only fit three into the space.

On the other hand, if you're not concerned with primo seats that make you feel like you're sitting on a cloud, then selecting chairs probably won't be as important to you as how many people you can comfortably accommodate in the theater. In this case, the situation becomes a numbers game. You might opt for a compact seating model to allow more chairs in the room. Likewise, if you decide the theater should seat eight, but it is straining to contain the wide chairs you have chosen, you might decide to cut the audience size to six, giving each guest more room to breathe. This is not to say that compact and comfortable seats are not out there. They do exist, but you need to approach the selection of chairs in this philosophical manner.

the chair-first approach

You've considered the available seating options and have selected a chair. All you have to do now is decide how you are going to orient the chairs in the room and then determine how many people the theater will comfortably hold. For example, if a chair is 40 inches (102 cm) wide and your room is 208 inches (5.3 meters) along the widest wall, you should be able to fit four chairs comfortably from left to right, with 4 feet (1.2 meters) of wiggle room. You must also make this calculation from the front and back of your room, taking into account viewing distance guidelines and figuring in legroom for the second row.

You can also incorporate risers to lift back rows a little higher off the ground than those in front. This imitates, on a smaller scale, the sloped seating of your local cineplex. Whether or not you can use risers depends on the height of your theater.

Consult with your guide to determine if your proposed seating arrangement will affect the technical aspects of the room (we'll get into that below).

Taking the chair-first approach doesn't mean you need a special degree to figure out seating arrangements; the job is really as simple as arranging your bedroom. Basically, the idea is to find what you think is comfortable and suitable. Generate several floor plans and decide which is best for you given your room's dimensions.

the audience-first approach

Another approach is to decide roughly how many people you would like the theater to seat given its dimensions, then determine what kind of seating you want. By figuring out how many people the theater should accommodate, you can easily determine the orientation of the seating and screen placement planning. Of course, your room may not accommodate all the people you want in the type of seating you want, so you may have to compromise. It is important to remain flexible during the planning stage, considering various floor plans, chairs, and audience sizes before committing to construction.

For example, say you want to fit eight people in the theater, four in each of two rows. If the theater chair you pick out is 36 inches (91 cm) wide, then the width of the wall your chairs are on will have to be, at the least, 36 times 4 inches (91 cm by 10 cm), which is 12 feet (3.7 meters), not including aisles or horizontal space between chairs. Say you want a 3-foot (0.9 meter) aisle on the left side of the room,

1 foot (0.3 meter) between each chair, and a 4-foot (1.2 meter) table in the middle of the four chairs on one row. Keep a running list of how many feet you will require to fit the rows of chairs or your sofa, then draw a layout to scale. Always add a couple of feet, at least, of wiggle room to cover unexpected snafus or unaccounted-for objects, such as a chair that must be pushed a few inches away from the wall to access an electrical outlet. The following calculations will give you an idea of how to account for space within a room. Remember, it is vital, before you put your seats into the floor plan, to include measurements for everything other than seating, such as an exposed gear rack at the rear of the theater, and the placement of closets, doorways, and windows. Extensive acoustical treatments, such as fabric walls to hide speakers or floating ceilings or floors may reduce the actual physical size of your room. Grab your graph paper and draw everything to scale. This will give you a realistic view of your possibilities.

< The glamour of the big screen comes home. A fiber-optic ceiling and star-themed wall-paper capture the magic of star-studded Hollywood.

Space Planning

calculation 1:
planning your theater, left-to-right dimensions

Say you have four separate theater chairs, each 36 inches (91 cm) wide. You would like to put them all in one row but want an aisle going down the left side of the room and a table in the middle of the row, with two chairs on each side. You would like the person in the rightmost chair not to feel cramped against the wall and want a little space between chairs. Keep a running list of how much space you will need to see if the arrangement is going to work.

4 CHAIRS @ 36 INCHES WIDE (91 CM) = 144 inches or 12 feet (3.7 meters)

AISLE = 3 feet (0.9 meter) on left side of room

TABLE = 4 feet (1.2 meters)

SPACE BETWEEN CHAIRS (1 foot between the two chairs not separated by the table) = 2 feet (0.6 meter)

SPACE BETWEEN WALL AND RIGHTMOST CHAIR = 2 feet (0.6 meter)

WIGGLE ROOM = 2 feet (0.6 meter)

TOTAL = 25 FEET (7.6 METERS)

Of course, if the longest wall of your existing room is less than 25 feet (7.6 meters), rethink your choices and room arrangement. Shop for a chair that is narrower or that comes in rows with shared armrests. As they do in full-size movie theaters, many home theater chairs come attached to one another so each seat shares an armrest, saving valuable real estate. Another solution is to put only three chairs on a row, leaving more room to play with.

calculation 2:
planning your theater, front-to-back dimensions

The same chairs we used in the previous example are 40 inches (102 cm) front to back. We want to see if we can fit two rows of seating comfortably in a room. The first consideration is the recommended viewing distance from the screen. You must also include the amount of space you want to have between rows. A typical movie theater puts 36 inches (91 cm) between one point on a row of chairs to the same point on the row behind it, which gives the audience member about 3 feet (0.9 meter) of legroom. In your dedicated home theater, you will probably want to give your guests at least 38 inches (97 cm) from one point on a row

to the same point on the previous row. Of course, if you choose theater loungers with recliners, allow room for those recliners when extended as well.

Do you want to have room behind the back row or want those chairs flush against the wall? Generally, sound is compromised if viewers' heads are against the rear wall. If you have inwall rear speakers, allow some breathing room away from your furniture. Again, keep a list of how much space you need, then draw it to scale.

DEPTH OF CHAIR = 40 INCHES (102 CM) X 2 ROWS = 80 inches (203 cm)

LEG ROOM BETWEEN BACK AND FRONT ROW = 38 inches (97 cm)

SPACE BETWEEN BACK WALL AND BACK ROW = 24 inches (61 cm)

SPACE BETWEEN FRONT WALL AND FIRST ROW = 144 inches (3.7 meters) (FOLLOW PLACEMENT GUIDELINES)

WIGGLE ROOM = 24 inches (61 cm)

TOTAL = 310 INCHES (A LITTLE OVER 25 FEET) (7.6 METERS)

If your room is not at least 26 feet (7.9 meters) from front to back, the two rows of the chairs we've discussed will not be feasible, and it's time to make compromises. You may reduce the amount of legroom between rows, or perhaps reduce legroom and put one row on a riser for a less cramped feeling in the back row. You might nip and tuck your screen size a bit, choosing a smaller screen in order to adhere to suggested viewing distances; this will allow the rows to be closer to the screen.

Most logically, reconsider your room orientation. Perhaps you want to flip-flop, making the room longer from front to back than it is wide, with more rows of fewer seats instead of two rows with many seats. In fact, if you put too many seats horizontally in front of the video image, the outer seats will have a poorer view of the screen and will receive slightly distorted audio because they are closer to the speaker on their side of the room rather than in the middle, the ideal listening and viewing position known as the sweet spot.

calculation 3:
planning your theater, top-to-bottom dimensions

This is where planning your theater can get tricky. When calculating top-to-bottom dimensions and how many rows of seats you can fit in your theater, you have to consider sightlines. We've all been to a theater that wasn't sloped, which meant you were sitting directly behind a person whose big head marred your view. This can happen in a dedicated theater as well.

Hence, many theater designers put the back rows of seating on risers. Some installers use 6 to 8 inches (15 to 20 cm) of carpeted wood to created a platform for the back chairs. Anything higher may require an extra stair. Say you are using the same chairs as in the previous examples and that they are 38 inches (97 cm) tall. You plan to install two rows of four seats with the back row on an 8-inch (20 cm) riser. How much headroom is desired, especially in the back row where guests are closer to the ceiling?

TALLEST RISER = 8 inches (20 cm)
HEIGHT OF CHAIR = 38 inches (97 cm)
DESIRED AUDIENCE HEADROOM IN BACK ROW WHEN SEATED
= 60 inches (152 cm)

TOTAL = 8 FEET 10 INCHES (2.65 METERS)

If your ceiling is not almost 9 feet (2.7 meters) high, you may have to reconsider the riser and try other techniques to prevent sightline problems, such as staggered seating so folks aren't sitting directly behind one another. Think about how much headroom you want when people are standing on the back riser. If your spouse is 6 feet (1.8 meters) tall and your room is, say, 9 feet (2.7 meters) high, you may not want to seat him on the back riser—or you may want to rethink your options.

Theater installers get even more specific with sightline measurements, taking into account the aspect ratio (see the sidebar on page 114) of the screen, the ideal viewing angle from the viewers' eyeballs, and more. One point to remember is that placing a screen higher makes it easier for people in the back row to see. If you place the screen lower on the wall, sightline problems are almost inevitable.

Designing your room can be challenging. Try various chairs, audience capacities, room orientation, and screen sizes to create the best room layout for you based on your lifestyle. Tinker with your measurements to determine your room's layout and where your chairs and screen should go. The project is a sort of puzzle. Don't worry; you'll know when the pieces fit right, and everything will fall into place. Remember, remain flexible.

design tip

the high life
If you are going to have tiered seating, with rows of seats on risers, place the screen higher rather than lower so the people in the back rows have an unobstructed view.

design tip

off center
Putting the seating along the longest wall of your theater is tempting, as you can fit more people closer to the screen and make your theater less deep. But avoid this temptation. The seating on the edges will be less than ideal, as the audience members in them will be closer to the surround-sound speakers and not in the middle of the sonic image, or the sweet spot. They will receive slightly distorted sound and will view the screen from an angle, which is bad viewing etiquette.

seat yourself: choosing home theater seating

Home theater seating options are as numerous as those for electronics. I've seen everything from checkered seats that mimic the colors of M&M candies to bright green faux leather sectionals. The first thing you need to determine, however, is the style of seating you are going to select, and by style I don't mean French versus Italian versus contemporary—I mean traditional theater seating versus traditional living room seating.

the traditional theater look

Theater seating creates a bona fide moviegoing atmosphere in the home and promotes ideal movie-watching body positions. Rows of red velvet seats, for example, are a throwback to the classic movie palaces of yore and leave no doubt that the purpose of the room is to watch movies.

A bevy of manufacturers specialize in creating comfortable, efficient theater seating. Because the seating is often the first thing people see when they enter a theater, it is important to make a good impression. Think about the feel of your theater. Do you want big, fluffy chenille seats or sleek black leather recliners? Consider the style, color, and features of each chair you encounter in your research. For example, some chairs have recliners, built-in cup holders, or built-in massage and control systems. Basically, however, there are three types of home theater seating: rows of theater seats, individual chairs, and reclining theater chairs.

v These Innovative Theaters brown leather chairs offer a traditional theater seating scheme but also evoke the comfort of a cozy brown leather couch.

> Theater furniture doesn't have to look so formal. In fact, it can look very fashionable. These seats, by Domus Design Collections, allow viewers to recline and enjoy the show.

design tip

a hollywood-style projection system

A Hollywood director wants to use his home theater to show dailies from the film he shot that day. To do this, he equips his theater with a film projector and hires a projectionist to run it, allowing him to enjoy films that have not been released theatrically.

rows of theater seats

The first and most common type of theater seating is rows of theater seats mounted to the floor. This approach can be more cost-effective than separate theater chairs because the seats share armrests, cutting down on manufacturing costs. This is often why you see theater seating in prices of separate (for just one chair), dual (two chairs together), and three-plus (three or more chairs strung together). Once you have decided you want two rows of three, for example, and you mount these seats on the floor, you automatically limit your flexibility in rearranging the room. Some theater seats come with optional floor plates (typically around $75 per chair) so they don't have to be mounted to the floor. That way, when you decide you don't like the view to the screen from the back row and want to build risers, you can do so without disassembling and reassembling the chairs.

stand-alone theater chairs

You can buy theater chairs (sometimes known as theater rockers) separately, but they tend to be expensive if you are going to have more than a couple of them. Again, the primary reason is the individual armrests. However, with stand-alone theater chairs you have a high degree of flexibility in placement. If the view from the back row isn't ideal, simply move the rocker over a few inches to clear the head of the person in front of you.

theater loungers

Theater loungers have a reclining option and can be bought in rows or as stand-alone units. Most offer at least two lounging options so viewers can adjust them to suit themselves. However, special considerations must be taken. For example, it might not be feasible to put theater loungers in the back row if legroom is limited.

do's and don'ts of theater chairs

The following do's and don'ts will help you in your search for the holy grail of home theater chairs.

v Many theater seats come with optional cupholders.

Do:

- Choose muted colors. A hot pink leather beanbag will reflect onto the screen, distorting the film's true colors.

- Choose a comfortable but firm chair. Soft chairs are great for the short haul, but for a four-hour double feature late at night, they might not provide the support your back needs, causing you to tire.

- Consider installing a side table for popcorn and drinks between chairs. You don't want guests to have to hold popcorn on their lap or set it on the floor when they're done enjoying it.

Theater floors are greasy for a reason! If a table is not an option, you might want to purchase chairs with cup holders or trays for easy snacking during a movie.

Don't:

- Try to cram in as many seats as possible; your prized room will feel cramped and uncomfortable.

- Choose fabrics that are light or hard to clean. Theater chairs are expensive and will be with you a long time. That coffee stain will stand

out more on a taupe chair than it will on a dark brown one.

- Skimp on your theater seating. It is a major focal point of the room and should make a statement. Once installed, it is not as easy to replace as, say, a DVD player or a framed movie poster.

- Choose a chair that has a high back; it will block sound coming from the surround speakers, prohibiting you from getting the full benefit of the surround experience.

> This theater has soft, brown chairs that match the decor of the home theater.

design tips

have a seat
Because of limited demand, few theater chair manufacturers have showrooms where you can test each chair. If you can find such a showroom, by all means take advantage of it. Manufacturers can send you swatches of the color you are interested in so you can see and feel the material. A lot of manufacturers allow you to choose your own fabric.

some assembly required
Some theater chairs are factory installed, but others require some assembly. Find out if the chair you're interested in comes with factory installation, and, if not, decide whether or not you are willing to install the chairs yourself. When installing theater chairs, allow about an hour for the first one and about thirty minutes for each chair after that.

protect your seats
When you have your chairs set up, apply industrial-grade fabric protector and allow two days for it to dry before sitting down. This will ensure your chairs have a long, happy life.

< This theater incorporates a
circular sofa in a soft beige
to evoke the feeling of a living
room in a dedicated theater.

∨ This casual room features
traditional sofas and ottomans
instead of regimented theater
chairs, giving the room a
relaxed, social environment.

living room style

Have you ever gone to a movie theater and been annoyed that you
can't put your feet up, that your legs feel cramped because the
seat in front of you is too close, that the armrest is immovable
and you want to stretch out? These are common movie theater
constrictions that need not be repeated in your home theater.
Designing a home theater in the style of a living room can make
you feel at home and offers a high degree of flexibility in furniture
choices, colors, fabrics, and placement. There is nothing wrong
with eschewing traditional theater seating for a less regimented
home theater environment that allows you to tailor your room to
suit your lifestyle. Some people like to lie down with a blanket
to watch a movie, or cuddle with their loved one, something you
can't necessarily do in a theater chair. If this is your style, choose
sofas and ottomans instead of chairs with armrests. You can even
put sofas or big, comfortable chairs on risers like theater seating
to avoid sightline problems.

Even when you take the casual living room route, remember you
are still creating a dedicated theater to watch movies in. Make
sure those couches aren't so comfortable that you'll be snoozing
during the opening credits. Also, tempting as it may be to place
traditional sofas at an angle from the screen so they face each
other, evoking the social spirit of a living room, try to avoid
doing so. The angles will cause eyestrain and neckstrain during
prolonged viewing sessions.

The casual look is less serious about its theatricality, so it lacks
the whimsical movie palace feel that reflects the room's dedicated
theater status. When it comes down to it, the style of seating you
choose is a matter of personal taste.

< Couches can be put on risers,
but remember to keep them
parallel to the screen. This
prevents neck pain caused
from viewing at an angle.

create a video plan

Now that you have selected your seating and how it is going to fit in the room, you want to start thinking about your gear—specifically, the video plan for your dedicated theater. We've talked a lot about various types of televisions and video displays that can be used in a small theater or media room. For a dedicated theater, where light can be completely controlled or eradicated and optimal video conditions created, it makes sense to invest in a front- or rear-projection system. These systems typically are more expensive than regular televisions, but they also provide larger images.

> Two CRT projectors light up the screen in this art deco theater. Viewers can choose from a wide range of seating options depending on their mood. Theater by Innovative Theaters.

projectors: the eyes of the dedicated theater

It is important to plan for your projector with care because it can be difficult to place in your room. Some projectors must be placed at a fixed length from the screen, so no floor plan is complete without positioning this important item. Don't go knocking down walls until you decide what kind of projector you want and where you are going to put it.

You can choose among many types of projectors, but generally, custom installers use two main types for dedicated home theaters: the cathode ray tube (CRT) projector and the digital light processing (DLP) projector. The CRT projector, which has three guns or tubes—one red, one blue, one green that, together, project an image onto a screen, is venerated by home theater installers the world over. Often, when a movie is shot without a lot of light, there is subtle detail in the shadows. CRTs are famous for their ability to reproduce shadow detail. In addition, they have excellent black levels. The black level of a projector is its ability to reproduce colors "below" black. A black-level control sets the light level of the darkest portion of the video signal to match that of the projector's black-level capability. Black is, of course, the absence of light. Many displays, however, have as much difficulty shutting off the light in the black portions of an image as they do creating light in the brighter portions. CRTs are also are incredibly bright, making them good choices for rooms with interfering ambient light, such as a media room.

However, CRTs have one feature that is sometimes problematic: They must be placed at a specific distance from the screen, so their placement is, therefore, inflexible. They also can weigh up to 250 pounds and are more cumbersome than DLP projectors. CRTs must be calibrated yearly to prevent drift in the image quality.

DLP projectors, on the other hand, have only one lens instead of three; this is nearly always a zoom lens, giving you a more flexible throw distance, or distance in which you can place the projector from the screen. In fact, it is desirable to place the DLP farther away from the screen so the light coming onto it is intensely concentrated. Plus, when you put the projector farther away from the screen, you use more of the lens's center. Light going through the edges of a lens can be distorted. By using more of the lens's center, you are improving image quality and minimizing distortion. Most projectors have fans that help keep them cool, given the enormous amount of light they pump out. DLP projectors have less fan noise than CRT projectors, as well. Recent improvements have been made in DLP projector technology; these days, their image quality competes with that of CRT technology.

It is better to mount both CRT and DLP projectors on the ceiling than on a table or in cabinetry near the seating area. If you place the projector on the floor, light coming from it bounces off the screen and onto the ceiling, dimming the image. Conversely, if you mount the projector on the ceiling, the light bounces off the screen and back at the viewer, making the image appear brighter. Plus, why utilize prime floorspace if you don't have to?

Regardless of the type of projector you choose, make sure it is capable of delivering a 16:9 aspect ratio for watching widescreen movies.

design tip

the imperfect square
For acoustic purposes, rooms that are square or near-square should be avoided. Try to find a room approximately 30 percent longer than it is wide.

projector mounts and lifts

Wherever you put your projector, concealing it is a good idea. An oblong box with hanging wires that dangles from your ceiling or sits on a coffee table in your home theater is not a pleasant sight to behold. You can hire a cabinetmaker to conceal the projector in a box that matches the ceiling so you can see it from the front of the room only, or you can have the projector fitted into a cabinet on the floor, again such that you can see it head-on only.

There are companies that specialize in motorized lifts and mounts that descend from the ceiling or rise from the floor so when the projector is not in use, you don't have to look at it. Similar lifts and cabinetry can be designed for practically any video display, including plasmas and direct-view and rear-projection televisions.

< This handsome theater has the feel of a dedicated theater, but when the video screen isn't being used, it rises up into the ceiling, showing off the homeowners' favorite movie posters and letting them enjoy the room as a sitting area.

screens like old times

A projector without a screen is like a ball without a mitt, a pitcher without a catcher. Projectors project light, but, contrary to popular belief, you can't see light until it lands on something. In fact, a light beam is the illumination of dust particles in the air or the atmosphere. For a projector to work, it must reflect the image either off or through some type of screen material. You can purchase screens for your projection system in any shape or size you want. Some roll up when you're not using them, others stay in a fixed position. You can even order custom screens that rise from a table or drop from the ceiling.

You will quickly discover that the shape of a movie changes from rectangular to square depending on the source material. The shape of the video image is called its aspect ratio. Some systems allow you to change the shape of the screen (or mask portions you aren't using) to fit the aspect ratio of the projected image. The size and shape that's best for you depends on your room, the distance between the viewers and the screen, the amount of ambient light in your room, the material you watch, and the type of projector you use.

High-gain screens reflect more light than the referenced material; they are a popular choice because they make the image appear brighter.

With this added apparent brightness comes a few tradeoffs, such as hot spots where the screen is brighter than in other areas. With a high-gain screen you also increase the possibility of a left-to-right color shift, depending on the type of projector you use. Negative-gain screens lower light output, which may improve black levels with bright projectors like DLP and CRT. Whichever type of screen you choose, remember that it is the last link in the video chain before the image reaches your eyes. Spending a lot of your budget on a projection video system and buying a bad screen doesn't make sense. If your screen is lousy, your image is going to be lousy.

Some screens for dedicated home theaters are acoustically transparent so you can place a center speaker directly behind the video image. That is, they have tiny holes that allow sound energy coming from a speaker to escape through the screen rather than bouncing off the screen and perhaps making the screen move. If you are going to put a center speaker behind your projection screen, a perforated screen is a must. Also select a screen offering good reflectivity, true color rendition, and strong contrast capability.

aspect ratio workshop

You've probably noticed the disclaimer before a theatrically released film being shown on television stating: "Notice: This film has been modified from its original version. It has been formatted to fit your screen." Movies have different aspect ratios than television programming. An aspect ratio is the relationship between the width and the height of a film image. A movie screen is much wider than it is tall, whereas a television screen is practically square. Aspect ratio is an ugly term, and, indeed, dealing with aspect ratios can get ugly. But if you understand them, they don't have to be scary.

At the beginning of motion picture history, all movies had pretty much the same shape; they all had an aspect ratio of 1.33:1, meaning the image was 1.33 times as wide as it was tall. In the 1930s, the Academy of Motion Pictures and Sciences made 1.33:1 (also known as 4:3) the official standard. Most classic films still have this aspect ratio. When it was time for the National Television Standards Committee (NTSC) to standardize the aspect ratio of television sets in the early 1950s, it made sense to make them the same shape as the majority of films being made.

Hollywood faced new competition when Americans started staying home to watch TV rather than going out to the movies. That's when Hollywood decided to change the way movies looked. They began experimenting with wide-screen aspect ratios, making films sometimes more than twice as wide as they were tall (2.35:1 aspect ratio). That's why, when you buy a DVD and bring it home to

watch on your 4:3 television, you see black bars below and above the video image. The long, skinny video images of today's films don't fit on our television sets any more. Half a century later, we are still making 1.33:1 sets, and almost all TV programming is the same.

When you are buying a television or projection screen, consider your priority—watching videos or watching TV—before deciding on the shape of your screen. If your priority is the former, buy a widescreen (16:9) set; if it is the latter, consider a 4:3 set.

When you want to watch a DVD that is not the same aspect ratio as your television set, you must change your television's settings to properly display the video image on the screen. For example, if you watch a 2.35:1 DVD on a 4:3 TV set without changing the settings, you'll notice people often resemble long, skinny, stretched aliens. That is because your TV is trying to squish the entire image onto your screen.

Another problem with watching widescreen DVDs on a 4:3 or standard set is that they're too wide to fit on a screen without cutting off the sides of the video image.

Letterboxing is the other option. Letterboxing shows the whole image on your TV but reduces it in size to fit on the screen, leaving some unused areas. This is when you see black bars on your TV. The director's original widescreen composition is preserved, and you aren't missing important parts of the video image. Some projection screens have masking systems that tailor the screen to the aspect ratio of the film.

> The black cloth surrounding this screen shows it has a masking system. This covers parts of the screen not being used, which varies depending on the DVD's aspect ratio.

create an audio plan

Creating an audio plan for your dedicated theater poses two challenges. The first is to integrate huge speakers into your room; the other, more complicated challenge is to tame your room's acoustics so your expensive speakers actually sound good. Just like in any other home theater, make sure to audition your speakers and consult a custom installer about which will fill your room with delightful sonic energy.

integrating speakers into a dedicated space

Dedicated theaters generally require large speakers, and most people building dedicated theaters prefer to have them hidden. After all, you don't go to the movie theater and walk around speakers or a subwoofer. Likewise, you want your home theater to be a room where all the technology that yields the awesome A/V experience is completely incognito—that is, unless you are making a statement with your gear. Architectural inwall speakers are one option, and can be discreetly hidden in walls and even covered with acoustic fabrics. If you don't want to tear holes in the wall, you can build a faux wall, sometimes called a fabric wall, that is basically erected for the sole purpose of putting in speakers. These faux walls are often covered with acoustically transparent fabric in a color that matches the decor of the room. Faux walls are used in many concrete structures, where boring into the walls isn't easy. Acoustic walls also act as a sort of diaphragm for rooms with a lot of resonance, absorbing some of the sound rather than reflecting it. However, no matter how many speakers you have, how big they are, where you put them, or how much you paid for them, they are only going to sound as good as the room you put them in. That is why an entire professional field is devoted to home theater room acoustics.

< Room acoustics vary depending on the type of room. A room with a lot of hard, reflective surfaces, like the one shown, might be acoustically "live," while a room with lots of damping materials, such fabric drapes, big pillows, and carpet, might be acoustically "dead."

design tip

bring source material with you

It has been said that home theater equipment looks and sounds as good as the material it is playing. For example, a TV at your local A/V retail chain may look stunning simply because the material on it is in high definition. Bring your own trusted test materials, such as DVDs and CDs, with you when you shop. This will help you determine the true nature of a component.

acoustic treatments

Dedicated theaters are usually designed from the outside in. Often remodels, the rooms usually are subject to their own preexisting conditions. That sounds like something you'd hear from your health insurance carrier, but acoustically, these rooms can indeed be sickly. Acoustic treatments are like the Band-Aids, or even the penicillin, of bad room acoustics. Fortunately, almost all acoustic ailments can be cured.

That isn't to say that administering the medicine is simple. In a dedicated home theater, room acoustics are even more important than in a small space. Room acoustics in a dedicated room depend on many factors, such as the position of the speakers and subwoofer, the shape of the room, the materials from which the room was constructed, and where a person is sitting within the room. It is wise to hire a certified room acoustician to diagnose your room and the dynamics of the sound within it. The job of a room acoustician is to provide ideal sonic conditions for as many people in the theater as possible.

After all, you don't want the only person in the theater enjoying the show to be the person sitting in the sweet spot.

Volumes can be written about the complex geometry of room acoustics, but we'll touch on the basics here so you get a rough idea of what to expect when trying to make your room sound great.

Many acousticians adhere to the principle of the LEDE room, or the live-end/dead-end room. A live space is usually composed of various hard, reflective surfaces and doesn't have a lot of fabric, carpet, or upholstered furniture to soften sound. A minimalist bachelor pad with hardwood floors and a glass coffee table might have live characteristics. A dead space, in contrast, is one where sound is more easily absorbed; its surfaces soak up rather than reflect sound. A carpeted bedroom with lots of heavy drapery, comforters, and fluffy pillows might sound dead.

For home theater, you want the dead end of the room to be in the front, where your video display is. A lot of important sound information is coming from your front three speakers. Keeping this area of the room dead, with few sonic reflections bouncing into the room, helps create an accurate soundstage and pinpoints details coming from your surround soundtrack.

Conversely, the live end of the theater should be at the rear of the room, by the rear speakers and seating area. This allows the information coming from the rear speakers to bounce forward to listeners' ears, creating an enveloping soundstage.

How dead the front and how live the rear of the room should be is largely a matter of personal preference. Some people find that listening to stereo music in a room that has a very dead front end is not as moving as listening to that same music in room with a slightly less dead front end.

Others insist on a completely dead front end for watching films. Experiment with various source materials, such as music versus movies, and decide how dead your front end should be. How you make your front end dead and your back end live is another discussion altogether. In a nutshell, there are basically two types of acoustic treatments you can purchase (or make yourself) for your room. Acoustic panels can be placed throughout the room to absorb sound and prevent it from reflecting in undesirable ways. Some acoustic panels come on stands; others are hung on the wall. These products come in various colors and fabrics, and some acoustic panel manufacturers even let you supply your own fabric to match the decor in your theater. Remember, when you are shopping for acoustic panels, the thicker they are, the more sound they absorb. Look for panels at least 2 inches (5 cm) thick to achieve the best results.

< It is usually desirable to keep the front end of the theater acoustically "dead," with more sound-absorbing than sound-reflecting material. These bookshelves on either side of the screen help diffuse sound.

> Acoustic diffusers can be placed at the rear of the room so that sound is reflected at different frequencies.

Diffuser panels can be placed at the rear of the room to spread out sound from your surround speakers. Some diffuser panels look amazing when exposed; they consist of a series of cubes at various depths on a panel that looks more like modern art than a room treatment. Diffuser panels also help minimize echo.

Bass traps are a godsend for anyone who can't whip their subwoofer into shape. Basically, these contraptions even out your room's bass response and absorb some of the excess energy coming from the subwoofer. You can also tinker with your subwoofer's placement to see where you get the best bass response from your room.

Now that you have a basic idea of the acoustic treatments out there that will help heal your room, you need to figure out where they go. The industry copes with panels by means of a well-known mirror trick. Start by having a friend sit in the sweet spot. Take a small mirror and walk around the front of the room until your friend can see a speaker in the mirror. Wherever he sees a speaker in the mirror, mark that place on the wall. Place an absorptive acoustic panel everywhere you make a mark. Deadening the front of the room is where things can get tricky. Start by placing absorptive panels behind your front speakers and adding diffusers to the sides. Listen to a well-known recording and notice how the music or movie changes as you move the acoustic panels. Tinker until you get the best sound.

Again, remember that the way your room sounds is largely personal, so don't feel tied down to the LEDE concept. There are many ways to make your room sound good. The bottom line is that you trust your own ears.

let there be light (or no light)

Lighting design is one of the most neglected areas of home theater design. Imagine sitting in your completely dark dedicated home theater you've already spent your daughter's college fund perfecting. When the movie is over you have to get up, stumble through the dark to the light switch, and flip on bright, relentless lights. You squint to try to let your pupils dilate slowly and are jerked back to reality like you're waking from a dream. Lighting can be an art in itself, and for home theater design, where lighting, and the lack thereof, are so important, it must be taken seriously to maximize the overall experience.

Lighting creates drama, contrast, mood, and atmosphere. And in a home theater, it not always what you see but what you don't see that counts. That is why theater lighting can be complicated. Before a film, mood lighting is nice, but in a dedicated theater, during a film the only light you want to see is that shining from your projector. Controlling the light between these phases is imperative.

In fact, designing lighting for a media room can be quite a challenge. To create ideal lighting architecture, you must develop a sense of what the space you want to light is about. A media room will be used for a variety of tasks other than watching films. You may, for example, want to do a crossword puzzle while your kids are watching Saturday morning cartoons. In a dedicated theater, you want lights that fade gradually in and out before and after a movie, giving your eyes time to wake up to the real world.

Once you get a feeling for the room's purpose(s), make a rough lighting floor plan that shows your lighting intentions. Three types of lighting come into play when designing a home theater: task lighting, accent lighting, and ambient lighting. Task lighting illuminates the performance of a specific duty, such as loading a disc into the DVD player or fixing a drink at the bar. This type of lighting should be focused and not spill into other areas of the room.

Accent lighting enhances features of a room, such as a sculpture or painting. This is the glamorous aspect of lighting design, where you can exercise artistic license. This is where drama and contrast come into play.

Ambient lighting, also known as filler lighting, fills in the areas between task and accent lighting and acts as the room's main lighting source. This type of lighting is often installed in the architectural features of a room, such as alcoves or soffits. To incorporate these lighting elements into your floor plan, first decide what tasks you will need to perform in the dark. It is sometimes helpful to have task lights flip on and off for convenience instead of merely programming them into your control system.

For accent lights, determine the focal point of the room when the lights are up (when the lights are down, the focal point, of course, will be the video screen) and where the artwork is going to go. Once you have determined accent and task lighting, you can decide how much ambient light you will need and where.

For example, John and Jane have a wonderful theater space with arched alcoves along the walls. They display their collection of antique vases in each alcove, and use accent lighting to enhance it. They install a crystal chandelier for ambient lighting when the theater is not in full video mode. The theater has tiers, so they need task lighting on the floors so guests don't trip when they get up, say, to go to the bathroom. A vintage *Casablanca* poster is in a framed marquee with bright bulbs around it. Five minutes before the movie starts, the control system gradually starts turning down the lights to signify the start of the film and to allow viewers' eyes to adjust. When the film is over, the lights come back up slowly over a period of five minutes. Lighting design is like the icing on the cake, and, as such, it must be prepared and executed with care.

Many types of lamps and bulbs can be used to create different lighting effects. Incandescent bulbs create a warm and inviting mood and are slightly yellowish in color, with some red tones. These lamps are great for lighting the seating area of your home theater because they help spread a cozy feeling. Halogen bulbs provide very clear light, slightly bluish in hue. A wide range of halogen bulbs is available in various shapes and sizes, making them easy choices for accent lights. Fluorescent lamps are known for lasting long; that's why you'll often find them in businesses, where stretching the dollar is key.

^ Lighting design, often
neglected in dedicated home
theaters, was not over ooked
in this Theo Kalomirakis
theater but, instead, made
into a design element of
the room.

This means a certain stigma is attached to them, but don't let that intimidate you. Fluorescents are now available in a wider range of color temperatures, so just avoid "office green." Their neutral density provides an ideal background light for watching a movie on a smaller screen, such as a direct-view monitor. Some home theater buffs call this a bias light. However, bias lights are not needed in dedicated home theaters.

Some lighting designers employ lenses that are fitted over lamps, and, much like a camera lens, change the way the light coming out of the lens looks. Lenses can block the light flow into specific areas and so can make highly effective task lighting. Say you want to be able to stir a drink at the bar while the movie is in full throttle. By fitting a lens over the halogen lamp at the bar, you can control its beam spread to just the area above the bar so it doesn't spill into the seating area. Soft-focus lenses make light appear softer.

> To pull off the ultimate home theater experience, planning is essential. Notice the chairs in this theater, by Atlanta Home Theater, are on risers and have plenty of legroom to spare. Take special consideration when you are figuring out where chairs should go in your room.

bias light

What your mom said about watching TV in the dark was true: It will hurt your eyes. The amount of light coming from a television screen is constantly changing, causing your pupils to practically pulsate with the amount of light going in and out of them. This can cause eye fatigue in as little as thirty minutes. When you are watching a small screen, you should have other light available throughout the room-bias light—preferably behind the screen, so as not to cause glare and reflections on the screen. This helps prevent eye fatigue.

In a dedicated theater, however, the screen surface is larger, and it alone should sufficiently illuminate your room. In fact, any projection system and screen should be viewed in complete darkness. When the projector is off, you shouldn't be able to see your hand.

fixture fixings

Styles of lamps, light fixtures, recessed lighting, and other lighting fixtures that hold a bulb are too numerous to discuss in detail, but for the purposes of home theater, it is often not how things are lit but what things are lit. You don't necessarily want to see the lighting fixtures at all. Remember, when you are looking at fixtures, flexibility is important; because the home theater space may be changed, the lights should have the capacity to be angled. Most of all, look for fixtures that fit your personal taste or the feel of your theater. If you have a themed theater, you might choose lighting to match.

Sconces are a popular lighting fixture choice in theaters when a film is not playing. You can find sconces in styles from art deco to Gothic to those with Admit One printed on them to give your room dramatic flair and provide ambient light. The trouble with recessed lighting is that it breaks the shell of the home theater room, which can allow sound to leak into other areas of the home. Sconces, which affix to walls rather than to the ceiling, emphasize the aisles of a theater and can be programmed to go up and down via the control system. Look for sconces not only through home theater furniture makers but also through traditional channels such as lighting boutiques and furniture stores. Some sconces can be customized; you can have your dedicated theater's name etched into them so that it is illuminated when the lights come up.

lighting control: the power of the touch panel

All those circuits that connect your lighting and make the room go from light to dark must be controlled. Many lighting control systems feature programmable controls that precisely adjust each lighting fixture to generate a predetermined lighting scheme that creates a certain mood. All you have to do is touch a button on the control panel, and the lights are taken to the set levels. There are a so wall-mounted controllers that allow you to do this. You can program drapes to coincide with lights and so forth, all through a touch panel control system.

> This *Titanic*-themed theater uses lighting to create a mood, a fiber-optic ceiling shows the stars as they were on the night the ship went down, and lamps light the way on the aisles.

design file

titanic ideas
Having fallen in love with James Cameron's film *Titanic*, a husband and wife decide to give their theater a theme based on the film and the tragic ship that inspired it. The theater's lobby has one wall painted with a mural of the ship. Inside, movie posters from the film featuring Kate Winslet and Leonardo DiCaprio grace the walls. Obtaining the exact latitude and longitude of the ship on the fated night it went down, the homeowners create a star-studded ceiling that recaptures the position of the cosmos using fiber optics.

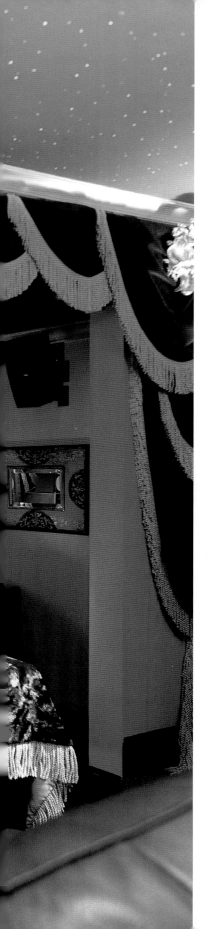

to theme or not to theme: that is the question

The dedicated home theater is a space designed with one thing in mind: entertainment. That is why many homeowners let their personalities flourish in these rooms. Dedicated theaters are often reserved for family use, are in more remote parts of the home, such as a basement or converted bedroom, and, therefore, aren't immediately accessible to guests, making homeowners less fearful of first impressions. Creating a theme for your home theater can be fun; however, think it through before you start painting clouds on the ceiling and rainbows and unicorns on the walls. Make sure your theme is something you won't grow tired of in the years to come; the last thing you want is to be stuck with a unicorn you have grown to hate.

> A themed theater lets your
imagination run wild. This
Moulin Rouge–inspired theater
features casual leather seating
and French luxury.

movie palace style

For design inspiration, some homeowners and interior designers
look to the classic movie palaces from the dawn of the movie
theater era. These theaters reflect the golden age of moviegoing,
when a night out at the movies was an experience in itself.
Their architects and designers traveled the world for inspiration,
and often combined various styles, from French to Italian to
Egyptian, to create an ornate and elaborate melting pot of styles.
The following accoutrements and fixtures in modern home
theaters find their roots in history and are a valuable source
of ideas for your own theater.

the marquee

Before television, there were movie theaters. In New York and Los Angeles, they cropped up one after the other in clusters and, therefore, often competed with one another for business. Those with the brightest lights and biggest names got the most attention—and the most business. The theater's marquee is where those bright lights and big names were displayed. Although homeowners have no competition, they still incorporate the marquee into their own theaters—often, above the doorway to the theater or in the theater lobby. Some families create their own names for their theater and broadcast them in bright lights.

∧ This dedicated home theater by Theo Kalomirakis incorporates the chandelier, ornate ceiling, columns, and red curtains of a classic movie theater.

the lobby

The lobby in the classic movie theaters of yore was the most elaborate room in the building. It usually featured chandeliers, red carpet—which can still be found at Hollywood movie premieres and awards ceremonies—high ceilings, ornate architecture, and towering columns. (The columns were needed to support the expansive roof of the theater's auditorium.)

∧ The Los Angeles Theater is an archetypal movie palace that many theater designers try to mimic, whether it be consciously or unconsciously.

< This theater pays homage to
the red curtain of the classic
movie houses by using curtains
in a deep brown to cover the
windows instead of the screen.

the proscenium

The proscenium is the arch over the stage in many theaters.
Often neglected in home theater design, an arch can be a
striking focal point for your theater. In the classic movie palaces,
the proscenium was where the design elements of the entire
theater melted together. Many of them were hand-carved from
wood, others were hand-painted.

the red curtain

Ever wonder why movie theaters have a red curtain over the
screen? The curtain is a relic of the days when movie palaces
were used for more than just showing films. Live vaudeville acts
with live music from the pipe organ were shown here, and the
curtain was needed for prop and costume changes and other
behind-the-scenes activities. We have, over the years, grown
accustomed to the red curtain and the drama it signifies.
You can incorporate automated curtains into your own theater,
but they don't have to be red. In fact, many homeowners give
their own individual spin to the curtain, choosing unconventional
fabrics and colors.

home theater from the ground up

Throughout this book, we have largely discussed retrofitting existing rooms with a home theater system. However, a whole world is devoted to creating theaters for homes at the blueprint stage. Of course, this is ideal, as perfect dimensions can be determined, windows simply eliminated, and the theater laid out perfectly. However, designing a room you can't see or hear is a major challenge. Atlanta Home Theater, a design firm based in Roswell,

Georgia, specializes in "muscle" home theaters and million-dollar home automation systems. In fact, they design projects only when they can get in at the ground level, when the blueprints are being drawn out and the theater is just a twinkle in the homeowner's eye.

Atlanta has a team of in-house designers who are familiar with the ins and outs of designing a home theater. They design prototypes of themed theaters and work in conjunction with the homeowner's own designers. If their client has their own

designer, they bring in that person at the planning phase to hammer out the details, set up a production timeline, and communicate with them consistently throughout the project. "Fabrics, furniture, color, dimension, accessories, and architecture all play as much of a role in the appeal of a home theater as does the system's performance," says Jennifer Ross, president of Atlanta Home Theater. From an interior design standpoint, comfort, according to Ross, is key. Lighting, color schemes, props, and accessories run a close second.

However, the professionals at Atlanta Home Theater are no strangers to challenges. "The challenge of home theater from the ground up is taking a nonexistent room, choosing the best system components in a fictitious space, and integrating them with the client's desired aesthetic environment without hindering the system's performance," says Ross.

When an interior designer is working with a custom installer, Ross suggests the designer learn as much as possible from the installer about the process.

Here is a list of helpful questions:

- How does your process work?
- What should I expect?
- What do you expect from me as a partner on this project?
- Is it more important for the client that the equipment be hidden or seen?
- Does the room require structural acoustic enhancement?
- Are there any special conditions or arrangements in this room that may affect the interior design?
- At what point is it appropriate to begin the interior design portion of the job?

One solution is to excavate the existing floor, along with several feet of concrete and dirt below it, and pour a new, lower concrete floor and install framing timbers. This gives the room more height and makes room for tiered seating.

Another option is to investigate what is above the ceiling to see if it can be raised. However, wiring or water pipes may have to be moved to do so, which can get expensive.

If neither the ceiling nor the floor can be moved, making tiered seating impractical, experiment with seating arrangements, such as slightly angling the chairs or couches diagonally instead of making them parallel to one another, giving everyone a clear line of sight to the screen. (If you angle them too much, you're asking for neck pain as you try to get a good viewing angle of the screen.)

design file

sunken treasures

The basement is a popular place to put a home theater. Basements are dark and often isolated from the rest of the home. Ideally, each row of seating in a home theater is on a different level. Risers are often built so audience members can see over each other's heads. Basements, however, often have height restrictions that make it difficult to comfortably accommodate two or more rows of people.

Resource Books and Magazines

Stereophile Guide to Home Theater
(323) 782-2000
www.guidetohometheater.com

Home Theater
(323) 782-2000
www.hometheatermag.com

Audio Video Interiors
(323) 933-9485
www.audiovideointeriors.com

Stereophile
(212) 229-4896
www.stereophile.com

Digital TV Magazine
(310) 589-7700
www.dtvmag.com

Company Contact Information

Atlanta Home Theater
(770) 642-5557

AVT
(925) 838-8444

Genesis Audio and Video
(949) 727-3700

Innovative Theaters
(310) 656-0065
www.innovativetheaters.com

TK Theaters
(212) 244-2404
(877) 858-4328
www.tktheaters.com

Wilson Home Theater Systems
(818) 716-9283
www.wilsonhometheater.com

All-Around Technology
(301) 656-5100

Audio Advice
(919) 881-2005
www.audioadvice.com

Herschelmann Designs
www.home-theater-guy.com

Acarian Systems
(631) 265-9577
www.alonbyacarian.com

Accusonic
(800) 523-2332
www.accusonicaudio.com

Acoustic Innovations
(800) 983-6233
www.acousticinnovations.com

Acoustic Room Systems (ARS)
(541) 942-7668
www.acousticroomsystems.com

Acoustic Sciences Corp.
(800) 272-8823
www.tubetrap.com

Acoustics First
(888) 765-2900
www.acousticsfirst.com

Adcom
(732) 683-2356
www.adcom.com

a/d/s/
(781) 729-1140
(800) 876-0800
www.adst.com

Aerial Acoustics Corp.
(781) 235-7715
www.aerialacoustics.com

Alpha-Core, Inc.
(203) 335-6805
www.alphacore.com

American Acoustic Development
(919) 876-2571
www.aadsound.com

Amplifier Technologies, Inc.
(888) 777-8507
www.ati-amp.com

AMX
(469) 624-8000
www.amx.com

Anthony Gallo Acoustics
(818) 341-4488
www.roundsound.com

Apature Products, Inc.
(904) 437-5530
www.apature.com

Aperion Audio
(888) 880-8992
www.aperionaudio.com

Apex Digital
(909) 930-0132

Armstrong/NXT
(442) 073-4350-50
www.nxtsound.com

Artcoustic
(949) 588-0075
www.artcoustic.com

Athena Technologies
(416) 321-1800
www.athenaspeakers.com

Atlantic Technology
(800) 922-2842
www.atlantictechnology.com

Atlantis Power/Exact Power
(530) 265-0981
www.exactpower.com

Audioaccess
(860) 346-0096
www.audioaccess.com

Audio Advisor
(616) 656-9587
www.audioadvisor.com

Audio Authority
(800) 322-8346
www.audioauthority.com

Audio Control
(425) 775-8461
www.audiocontrol.com

Audio Design Associates, Inc.
(914) 946-9595
www.ada-usa.com

Audio Note
(302) 658-8876

Audio Plus Services
(800) 663-9352
www.audioplusservices.com

Audio Pro America
(818) 889-3244

Audio Products Int'l. (API)
(416) 321-1800

Audio Research
(763) 577-9700
www.audioresearch.com

Audio Video Multimedia Solutions
(636) 978-8173
www.avmsolutions.com

Audio Video Source
(818) 701-9073
www.avxi.com

Audiophile Systems
(888) 272-2658
www.audiophilesystems.com

AudioQuest
(949) 585-0111
www.audioquest.com

Auralex
(317) 842-2600
www.auralex.com

AuraSound
(800) 909-AURA
www.aurasound.com

Aurex Corporation
(800) 918-8804

Auton
(661) 257-9282
www.auton.com

AV Link
(714) 990-1858
www.avlinkinc.com

AVM Solutions
(800) 531-6886
www.sanibelsound.com

Axiss
(310) 329-0187
www.axiss.com

Bag End Loudspeakers
(847) 382-4550
www.bagend.com

Balanced Audio Technology
(800) 255-4228
www.balanced.com

Bang and Olufsen
(847) 590-4900
UK: (44) 118 969 2288
www.bang-olufsen.com

Barco
(770) 218-3200
www.barco.com

Bel Canto
(612) 317-4550

Bell'O International LLC
(732) 972-1333
www.bellointl.com

Better Cables
(877) 433-7039
www.bettercables.com

BIC
(888) 461-4628
www.bicamerica.com

Billy Bags Designs
(805) 644-2185
www.billybags.com

B&K Components, Ltd.
(800) 543-5252
www.bkcomp.com

Blue Circle Audio
(519) 469-3215
www.bluecircle.com

Bose
(508) 879-7330
UK: (44) 800 085 9021
www.bose.com

Bostronics Corporation
(888) 466-9262

Boulder Amplifiers
(303) 449-8220
www.boulderamp.com

Bright Star Audio
(805) 375-2629

Bryston Ltd/East
(705) 742-5325
www.bryston.ca

B&W Loudspeakers
(978) 664-2870
www.bwspeakers.com

Caig Laboratories
(858) 486-8388
www.caig.com

Canare
(818) 365-2446
www.canare.com

California Audio Technology
(888) 432-7228
www.calaudiotech.com

Cambridge SoundWorks, Inc.
(800) 367-4434
Outside US: (978) 623-4400
www.cambridgesound
works.com

Camelot Technology
(215) 357-8356
www.camelot-tech.com

Canton
(612) 706-9250
www.cantonusa.com

Cardas Audio
(541) 347-2484
www.cardas.com

Cary Audio Design
(919) 481-4494
www.caryaudio.com

Celestion
(732) 683-2356
www.celestion.com

Cerwin-Vega
(805) 584-9332
www.cerwin-vega.com

Channel Master
(919) 934-9711
www.channelmaster.com

Channel Plus
(714) 996-4100
www.channelplus.com

Channel Vision
(800) 840-0288
www.channelvision.com

Checkpoint (SAS)
(310) 891-1550
www.checkpoint.com

Chisholm
(408) 559-1111
www.chisholm.com

Cinema Quest, Inc.
(303) 3740-7278
www.ideal-lume.com

Citation
(860) 346-0896

Clark Synthesis
(800) 898-1945
www.clarksynthesis.com

Classé Audio Inc.
(514) 636-6384

Clements Loudspeakers
(480) 899-3565
www.clements-prc.com

Coincident Speaker Technology
(905) 886-6728
www.coincidentspeaker.com

Communications Specialties, Inc.
(631) 273-0404
www.commspecial.com

conrad-johnson
(703) 698-8581
www.conradjohnson.com

Convergent Audio Technology
(716) 359-2700

Craig
(310) 926-9944

Creative Labs
(408) 546-6465
www.soundblaster.com

Crestron
(201) 767-3400
wwww.crestron.com

Crystal View
(888) 388-2022
www.crystalviewinc.com

Current Designs
(201) 342-1235
www.current-designs.com

D-Box Audio, Inc.
(450) 442-3003

Da-Lite Screen Company
(800) 622-3737
www.da-lite.com

DCM Loudspeaker
(877) 326-5683
www.dcmspeakers.com

Definitive Technology
(410) 363-7148
www.definitivetech.com

Delta Products Corporation
(503) 533-8444

Denon
(973) 396-0810
www.del.denon.com

Digital Projection
(770) 420-1365
www.digitalprojection.com

Digitools
(925) 681-2326
www.d-tools.com

DigiVision
(858) 571-4700

Discovery Cable
(305) 744-9903

Dish Network
(800) 333-DISH
www.dishnetwork.com

Display Devices, Inc.
(303) 412-0399
www.displaydevices.com

Divergent Technologies, Inc.
(519) 749-1565
www.divergent.com

DDC—Domus Design Collection
(212) 685-0800
www.ddcnyc.com

Draper Shade and Screen
(765) 987-7295
www.draperinc.com

DreamVision
(800) 871-2920

Dukane
(800) 676-2485
www.dukane.com

Dunlavy Audio Lab, Inc.
(719) 592-1159
www.dunlavyaudio.com

Dwin Electronics, Inc.
(818) 239-1500
www.dwin.com

Dynaco
(631) 434-1200
www.dynaco.com

Dynaudio North American
(630) 238-4200
www.dynaudiousa.com

Earthquake
(650) 327-3003
www.earthquakesound.com

EAS Incorporated
(780) 418-1528
www.avrak.com

Echo Busters
(888) ECHO-BUST
www.echobusters.com

Equi-tech
(877) EQUITEC
www.equitech.com

Elac
(909) 686-6301
www.elac.com

ELAN Home Systems
(859) 269-7760
www.elanhomesystems.com

Electrograph
(631) 436-5050
www.electrograph.com

Elite Video
(781) 938-6606
www.elitevision.com

Energy Speaker Systems
(416) 321-1800
www.energy-speakers.com

Enlightened Audio Design
(641) 472-4312
www.eadcorp.com

EOSS
(562) 809-8630
www.soundpoles.com

Equity Group
(800) 370-3740

Escient
(317) 571-1111
www.escient.com

Esoteric Audio
(800) 225-5689
www.esotericaudio.com

Extron
(800) 633-9876
www.extron.com

Faroudja
(408) 735-1492
www.faroudja.com

Flat Panel
(213) 617-9006
www.fpshifi.com

Focus Enhancements
(408) 866-8300
www.focusinfo.com

Focus Systems
(408) 866-8300
www.focusinfo.com

Fortress
(909) 627-4270
www.fortresseating.com

Fosgate Audionics
(866) 777-7282
www.fosgateaudionics.com

Fujitsu
(888) 888-3424
www.plasmavision.com

Furman Sound
(707) 763-1010
www.furmansound.com

Gemini
(973) 471-9050
www.gemini-usa.com

Genelec
(508) 652-0900
www.genelec.com

Goldline
(203) 938-2588
www.goldline.com

Go Video
(408) 588-8000
www.govideo.com

Green Mountain Audio
(719) 636-2500
www.greenmountainaudio.com

Grundig
(650) 361-1611
www.grundigradio.com

Gryphon Audio
(458) 689-1200
www.gryphon-audio.com

The Guitammer Company
(888) 676-2828
www.guitammer.com

Hafler
(888) HAFLER-1
www.halfer.com

Harman/Kardon
(800) 422-8027
www.harmankardon.com

Harmonic Technology
(858) 486-8386
www.harmonictech.com

Hitachi America Ltd.
Home Electronics Division
(619) 661-0227
www.hitachi.com/tv

HSU Research
(714) 666-9260
www.hsuresearch.com

Hughes Network Systems
(800) 274-8995
www.hns-usa.com

I.O. Display Systems
(650) 323-8407

IEV International
(800) 438-6161
www.iev.com

IKEA
(800) 434-4532
www.ikea.com

Illbruck/Sonex
(612) 521-3555
www.illbruck-sonex.com

Inca
(310) 808-0001
www.inca-tvlifts.com

Induction Dynamics
(913) 663-9770
www.inductiondynamics.com

Infinity Systems, Inc.
(800) 553-3332
www.harman.com

InFocus
(503) 685-8888

Inline
(714) 921-4100
www.inlineinc.com

Innovative Audio
(800) 595-7757
www.innovativeaudiousa.com

Intech Audio Video
(516) 931-6800
www.intechav.com

Integra
(800) 225-1946
www.integrahometheater.com

Interact
(410) 785-5661

Invisisound
(415) 840-2000
www.monstercable.com

ISCO Optic
(877) ISCO-USA
www.asa-reps.com

Izahi Corp.
(650) 326-7285
www.izahi.com

James Loudspeaker
(520) 854-3740
www.jamespeaker.com

Jamo
(847) 465-0005
www.jamospeakers.com

JBL
(516) 496-3400
www.jbl.com

Jensen
(407) 333-0900
www.jensen.com

JMlab
(800) 663-9352
www.focal-fr.com

Joseph Audio
(800) 474-4434
www.josephaud.com

JVC
(973) 315-5000
UK: (44) 870 330 5000
www.jvc.com

KEF
(732) 683-2356
www.kef.com

Kenwood USA
(800) KENWOOD
www.kenwoodusa.com

Key Digital
(718) 796-7178
www.keydigital.com

Kimber Kable
(801) 621-5530
www.kimber.com

Kinergetics
(323) 981-1678

Klipsch
(800) KLIPSCH
www.klipsch.com

Knoll Systems
(604) 272-4555
www.knollsystems.com

Krell
(203) 799-9954
www.krellonline.com

Legacy Audio
(217) 544-3178
www.legacy-audio.com

Legend Audio
(800) 750-3030
www.legendaudio.net

Leviton
(425) 485-5100
www.leviton.com/lin

Lexicon, Inc.
(781) 280-0300
www.lexicon.com

Liberty Wire and Cable
(719) 260-0061
www.libertycable.com

Lightolier Controls
(508) 679-8131
www.lightolier.com

Linn, Inc.
(904) 645-5242
www.linninc.com

LiteTouch
(801) 486-8500
www.litetouch.com

Loewe
www.loewe.de

Lucasey
(800) LUCASEY
www.lucasey.com

Luce
(954) 421-5330
www.lucetv.com

Lucifer Lighting
(800) 879-9797
www.luciferlighting.com

Lutron Electronics
(610) 282-3800
www.lutron.com

M&K Sound
(818) 701-7010
www.mksound.com

Magnepan
(800) 474-1646
www.magnepan.com

Magnum Dynalab
(800) 551-4130
www.magnumdynalab.com

Marantz
www.marantz.com

Marsh Sound Design
(415) 927-4672
www.marshsounddesign.com

MartinLogan
(785) 749-0133
www.martinlogan.com

MB Quart
(508) 668-8973
www.mbquart.com

MBL of America
(480) 563-4393
www.mbl-hifi.com

McCormack Audio
(703) 573-9665
www.mccormackaudio.com

McIntosh
(607) 723-3512
www.mcintoshlabs.com

Meadowlark Audio
(760) 598-3763
www.medowlarkaudio.com

Meridian
(404) 344-7111
www.meridian-audio.com

Mirage Speakers
(416) 321-1800
www.miragespeakers.com

Mitsubishi Digital Electronics
America, Inc.
(800) 332-2119
www.mitsubishi-tv.com

Mondial Designs Ltd.
(866) 781-7284
www.mondialdesigns.com

Monitor Audio USA
(905) 428-2800
www.monitoraudio.com

Monivision
(714) 893-8113
www.monivision.com

Monster Cable
(415) 840-2000
www.monstercable.com

Mordaunt-Short
www.mordaunt-short.com

Morel
(800) MOREL-14
+972.8.9301161
www.morelhifi.com

Motorola SPS
(858) 455-1500
www.gi.com

MSB Technology
(650) 747-0400
www.msbtech.com

MTX
(800) 225-5689
www.mtxaudio.com

Muse Electronics
(714) 554-8200
www.museelectronics.com

Music Hall
(516) 487-3663
www.musichallaudio.com

Musical Fidelity
(905) 428-2800
www.musical-fidelity.com

NAD Electronics
(781) 784-8586
www.nadelectronics.com

Nagra USA, Inc.
(800) 813-1663
www.nagrausa.com

Naim Audio
www.naim-audio.com

Nakamichi America Corp.
(310) 631-2122
www.nakamichi.com

NCT Audio Products, Inc.
(203) 226-4447
www.nctgroupinc.com

NHT
(407) 333-0900
www.nhthifi.com

Niles Audio Corporation
(305) 238-4373
www.nilesaudio.com

Nordost Corp/Flatline Cable
(508) 879-1242
www.nordost.com

Numark
(401) 295-9000
narruda@numark.com

Odyssey
(317) 299-5578
www.odysseyaudio.com

Omnimount Systems
(480) 829-8000
www.omnimount.com

Onkyo USA
(800) 229-1687
www.onkyousa.com

Outlaw Audio
(877) 688-5292
www.outlawaudio.com

Ovation
(508) 481-9930
www.ovation.com

Owens Corning
www.owenscorning.com

Panamax
(800) 472-5555
www.panamax.com

Panasonic
(800) 211-PANA
www.panasonic.com

Panel Fold
(305) 688-3501
www.panelfold.com

Paradigm
(905) 632-0180
www.paradigm.com

Parasound
(415) 397-7100
www.parasound.com

Path Group
(480) 539-8000
www.path.co.uk

Piega
www.sanibelsound.com

Performance Media Industries
(PMI)
(415) 454-2087
www.pmiltd.com

Perpetual Technologies
(303) 543-7500
www.perpetualtechnologies.com

Phase Technology
(888) 742-7385
www.phasetech.com

Philips Consumer Electronics
(800) 531-0039
UK: 0870 900 9070
www.philips.com

Phoenix Gold
(503) 978-8505
jfornos@phoenixgold.com

Pinnacle Loudspeakers
(516) 576-9052
www.pinnaclespeakers.com

Pioneer Electronics
(213) 746-6337
www.pioneerelectronics.com

Plateau Corp.
(519) 443-6122
www.plateaucorp.com

Plus
(201) 818-2700
www.plushometheater.com

Polk Audio
(410) 358-3600
www.polkaudio.com

Princeton Graphics
(800) 747-6249
www.princetonhdtv.com

Pro Audio Ltd.
(847) 526-1660

Proficient
(909) 787-9940
www.proficientaudio.com

Proton
(562) 404-2222
www.proton-usa.com

PS Audio
(720) 406-8946
www.psaudio.com

PSB Speakers
(781) 784-8586
www.psbspeakers.com

Red Rose
(212) 628-5777
www.redrosemusic.com

RBH
(800) 543-2205
www.rbhsound.com

Recoton Home Audio
(407) 333-8900
www.recoton.com

Replay TV
(650) 210-1000
www.replaytv.com

Revox
(770) 442-2697
www.revox.com

RGB Spectrum
(510) 814-7000
www.rgb.com

Richard Gray's Power Company
(800) 880-3474
www.richardgrayspower
company.com

Rip-Tie
(415) 543-0170
www.rip-tie.com

RKR Video
(714) 594-0548
www.rkrvideo.com

Rotel
(978) 664-2870
www.rotel.com

RPG Diffusor Systems
(301) 249-0044
www.rpginc.com

Runco
(510) 293-9154
www.runco.com

Russound
(603) 659-5170
www.russound.com

Sampo Corp. of America
(626) 856-3348
www.sampoamericas.com

Samsung
(800) SAMSUNG
www.samsung.com

Sanyo Fisher
(818) 998-7322
www.fisherav.com

Sencore
(605) 339-0100
www.sencore.com

Sensory Science
(480) 905-9621
www.sensoryscience.com

Sharp Electronics
(800) BE-SHARP
www.sharpelectronics.com

Sherbourne
(978) 663-7385
www.sherbourne.com

Sherwood America
(800) 962-3203
www.sherwoodusa.com

Signature Wire
(303) 715-1515
www.signaturewire.com

Silicon Image
(408) 616-4000
www.siimage.com

SIM2
(954) 442-2999
www.sim2.com

Sima Products Corp.
(412) 828-3700
www.simacorp.com

Simaudio Ltd.
(800) 345-7462
www.simaudio.com

SLS Loudspeakers
(417) 883-4549
www.slsloudspeakers.com

Snell Acoustics
(978) 373-6114
www.snellacoustics.com

Snell and Wilcox
(212) 675-9720
www.snellwilcox.com

Soliloquy
(919) 876-7554
www.solspeak.com

Solus Architectural Audio
(480) 899-3565
www.solus-prc.com

Sonance
(800) 582-7777
www.sonance.com

SONICblue
(408) 588-8000

Sonic Frontiers
(905) 828-4575
www.sonicfrontiers.com

Sonic Integrity
(562) 944-3499

Sony
(800) 222-SONY
UK: (44) 1923 819630
www.sony.com

Sound Advance Systems
(714) 556-2378
www.soundadvance.com

Sound Dynamics
(416) 321-1800
www.sound-dynamics.com

Soundcraftsmen
(815) 232-2000

Soundstream
(323) 724-4600

Spatializer
www.spatializer.com

SpeakerCraft
(909) 787-0543
www.speakercraft.com

Spectral, Inc.
(408) 738-8521

SRS Labs
(949) 442-1070

SSI
(626) 305-0500
www.ssihtp.com

Status Acoustics
(800) 543-2205
www.statusacoustics.com

StereoStone
(800) 350-7866
www.stereostoneinc.com

Stewart Filmscreen
(800) 762-4999
www.stewartfilm.com

Straight Wire
(954) 925-2470
www.straightwire.com

Studio Experience
(800) 667-6147
www.studioexperience.com

StudioTech
(800) 887-8834
www.studiotech.com

Sumiko
(510) 843-4500
www.sumikoaudio.com

Sunfire
(425) 335-4748
www.sunfire.com

SVS, Inc.
(303) 766-9505
www.svslifts.com

Synergistic Research
(949) 642-2800
www.synergisticresearch.com

TacT Audio, Inc.
(201) 440-9300
www.tactaudio.com

Tag McLaren
(888) 293-9929
www.tagmclaren.com

Tannoy/T.G.I. North America
(519) 745-1158
www.tannoy.com

TARA Labs
(541) 488-6465
www.taralabs.com

TAW (Theater Automotion Wow)
(407) 363-5365
www.tawinc.net

TEAC
(323) 726-0303
UK: + 44 (0) 1923 819630
www.teac.com

Ten-Lab
(818) 706-8120
www.tenlab.com

Terk
(631) 543-1900
www.terk.com

Theatre Design Associates
(312) 829-8703
www.theatredesign.com

Theo Kalomirakis Theaters
(877) 858-4328
www.tktheaters.com

Theta Digital
(510) 339-3404

Thiel Audio
(859) 254-9427
www.thielaudio.com

Thomson Multimedia
(800) 336-1900
www.rca.com

TiVo
(877)-FOR-TIVO
www.tivo.com

Toshiba
(201) 628-8000
UK: 0800 444 8944
www.toshiba.com

Transparent Audio, Inc.
(207) 284-1100
www.transparentcable.com

Triad Speakers
(800) 666-6316
www.triadspeakers.com

Tributaries
(800) 521-1596
www.tributariescable.com

Ultimate Sound, Inc.
(909) 594-2604
www.ultimate-sound.com

Ultralink Products, Inc.
(909) 937-1073
www.ultralinkcables.com

Universal Remote Control, Inc.
(914) 235-2610
www.hometheatermaster.com

Uniview
(972) 233-0900
www.uniview.net

Unisound
(626) 458-9812
www.unisound.com

VAC/Valve Amplification
Company
(919) 596-1107
www.vac-amps.com

Vacuum Tube Logic
(909) 627-5944
www.vtl.com

Vampire Wire
(813) 948-2707
www.vampirewire.com

Vandersteen Audio
(559) 582-0324
www.vandersteen.com

Vantage
(801) 229-2800
www.vanltg.com

Velodyne Acoustics
(408) 436-7270
www.velodyne.com

Vergence Technology
(707) 751-0270
www.vergenceaudio.com

Vialta
(510) 870-3088
www.vialta.com

Video Essentials
www.videoessentials.com

Video Display Corporation
(321) 784-4427
www.vdcdisplaysystems.com

Wadia Digital
(925) 875-9495
www.wadia.com

Wegg3
(310) 577-9148
www.wegg3.com

Westlake Audio
(805) 499-3686
www.westlakeaudio.com

Wharfedale
(781) 440-0888
www.wharfedale.com

Whise Precision Audio
61.3.9763.9111
www.whise.com.au

Wilson Audio
(801) 377-2233
www.wilsonaudio.com

Winegard
(319) 754-0675
www.winegard.com

Wireworld by David Salz, Inc.
(954) 962-2650
www.wireworldaudio.com

Xantech
(818) 362-0353
www.xantech.com

Yamaha
(714) 522-9105
UK: (44)1923 233166
www.yamaha.com

Zenith Electronics
(847) 391-7000
www.zenith.com

Zoran
(408) 919-4280
www.zoran.com

Antennas

Channel Master
(919) 934-9711
www.channelmaster.com

Terk Technologies
(631) 543-1900
www.terk.com

Winegard
(319) 754-0600
www.winegard.com

Auxiliary Switchers and Transcoders

Audio Authority
(800) 322-8346
www.audioauthority.com

EMM Labs
(403) 225-4161
www.emmlabs.com

Extron
(800) 633-9876
www.extron.com

Key Digital
(888) 258-2028
www.keydigital.com

MSB
(650) 747-0400
www.msbtech.com

R.E. Designs
(781) 592-7862
www.redesignsaudio.com

Crossovers

AudioControl
(425) 775-8461
www.audiocontrol.com

Bag End
(847) 382-4550
www.bagend.com

Bryston
(705) 742-5325
www.bryston.ca

HSU Research
(714) 666-9260
www.hsuresearch.com

Krell Industries
(203) 799-9954
www.krellonline.com

M&K
(818) 701-7010
www.mksound.com

Outlaw Audio
(866) 688-5292
www.outlawaudio.com

Parasound
(866) 770-8324
www.parasound.com

Rane
(425) 355-6000
www.rane.com

Zoran
(408) 919-4280
www.zoran.com

Equalizers

AudioControl
(425) 775-8461
www.audiocontrol.com

Kenwood
(800) KENWOOD
www.kenwoodusa.com

Perpetual Technologies
(303) 543-7500
www.perpetualtechnologies.com

Rane
(425) 355-6000
www.rane.com

Sony
(800) 222-SONY
UK: 08705 111999
www.sony.com

Yamaha
(714) 522-9105
UK: (44) 1923 233166
www.yamaha.com

Power Enhancers

Atlantis Power/ExactPower
(800) 663-9352
www.audioplusservices.com

Audio Power Industries
(714) 545-9495
www.audiopower.com

Equi=Tech
(877) EQUITECH
www.equitech.com

Furman Sound
(707) 763-1010
www.furmansound.com

Monster Cable
(415) 840-2000
www.monstercable.com

Panamax
(800) 472-5555
www.panamax.com

PS Audio
(720) 406-8946
www.psaudio.com

Quantum
(800) 809-5480
www.quantumqrt.com

Richard Gray's Power Company
(800) 880-3474
www.richardgrayspower
company.com

Tice Audio
(561) 575-7577
www.ticeaudio.com

RF Distribution

ChannelPlus
(800) 999-5225
www.channelplus.com

Channel Master
(919) 934-9711
www.channelmaster.com

Channel Vision
(800) 840-0288
www.channelvision.com

Lutron
(610) 282-3800
www.lutron.com

Room Acoustics

Acoustic Innovations
(800) 983-6233
www.acousticinnovations.com

Acoustics First Corporation
(888) 765-2900
www.acousticsfirst.com

Acoustic Sciences Corporation
(800) 272-8823
www.tubetrap.com

ARS (Acoustic Room Systems)
(541) 942-7668
www.acousticroomsystems.com

Auralex Acoustics
(317) 842-2600
www.auralex.com

Echo Busters
(631) 242-6100
www.echobusters.com

Illbruck
(612) 521-3555
www.illbruck-sonex.com

Kinetics Noise Control
(614) 889-0480
www.kineticsnoise.com

Owens Corning (See also ARS)
(800) GET-PINK
www.owenscorning.com

PAC International
(503) 649-7700
www.pac-intl.com

Panel Fold
(305) 688-3501
www.panelfold.com

Performance Media Industries
(PMI)
(415) 454-2087
www.pmiltd.com

RPG Diffusor Systems
(301) 249-0044
www.rpginc.com

Theatre Design Associates
(312) 829-8703
www.theatredesign.com

TK Theaters (Theo Kalomirakis)
(212) 244-2404
(877) 858-4328
www.tktheaters.com

Setup Tools

Audio Advisor
(616) 656-9584
www.audioadvisor.com

Checkpoint (SAS)
(310) 891-1550
www.checkpoint3d.com

Gold Line
(203) 938-2588
www.gold-line.com

Ovation Software (Avia)
(508) 481-9930
www.ovation.com

Performance Media Industries
(PMI)
(415) 454-2087
www.pmiltd.com

Radio Shack
(800) THE SHACK
www.radioshack.com

Sencore
(605) 339-0100
www.sencore.com

Sensory Science Corporation
(408) 588-8000
www.sensoryscience.com

Synergistic Research
(949) 642-2800
www.synergisticresearch.com

Video Essentials
(Joe Kane Productions)
www.videoessentials.com

Speaker and Line-Level Cables

Acoustic Research
(407) 333-8900
www.acoustic-research.com

Apature Products
(904) 437-5530
www.apature.com

AudioQuest
(949) 585-0111
www.audioquest.com

A/V Link
(714) 990-1858
www.avlinkinc.com

Belden
(800) 235-3361
www.belden.com

Belkin
(310) 898-1100
www.belkin.com

BetterCables
(877) 433-7039
www.bettercables.com

Blue Circle Audio, Inc.
(519) 469-3215
www.bluecircle.com

Canare
(818) 365-2446
www.canare.com

Cardas Audio
(541) 347-2484
www.cardas.com

Coincident Speaker Technology
(905) 660-0800
www.coincidentspeaker.com

Esoteric Audio USA
(800) 806-6111
www.esotericaudio.com

Gemini
(973) 471-9050
www.gemini-usa.com

Harmonic Technology
(858) 486-8386
www.harmonictech.com

IXOS
(480) 539-8000
UK +44 (0) 1844 219000
www.path.co.uk

Kimber Kable
(801) 621-5530
www.kimber.com

Liberty Wire and Cable, Inc.
(719) 260-0061
www.libertycable.com

MIT, Inc.
(916) 625-0129
www.mitcables.com

Monster Cable Products, Inc.
(415) 840-2000
www.monstercable.com

Musical Fidelity
(905) 428-2800
www.musical-fidelity.co.uk

Nordost
(508) 881-1116
www.nordost.com

Parts Express
(800) 338-0531
www.partsexpress.com

Radio Shack
(800) THE SHACK
www.radioshack.com

Recoton Home Audio
(407) 333-8900
www.recoton.com

R.E. Designs
(781) 592-7862
www.redesignsaudio.com

Russound
(603) 659-5170
www.russound.com

Signature Wire
(888) 715-1555
www.signaturewire.com

Straight Wire
(954) 925-2470
www.straightwire.com

Synergistic Research
(949) 642-2800
www.synergisticresearch.com

TARA Labs
(541) 488-6465
www.taralabs.com

Transparent Audio
(207) 284-1100
www.transparentcable.com

Tributaries Cable
(800) 521-1596
www.tributariescable.com

Ultralink Products, Inc.
(909) 937-1073
www.ultralinkcables.com

Vampire Wire
(813) 948-2707
www.vampirewire.com

Westlake Audio
(805) 499-3686
www.westlakeaudio.com

WireWorld Cable
(954) 680-3848
www.wireworldaudio.com

Furniture

Bass Industries
(800) 346-8575
www.bassind.com

Lighting

CinemaQuest, Inc.
(Ideal-Lume)
(303) 740-7278
www.ideal-lume.com

Crestron
(888) CRESTRON
www.crestron.com

ImageCrafters, Inc.
(508) 947-0420
www.imagecraftersinc.com

Leviton
(800) 833-3532
www.leviton.com

Lightolier Controls
(508) 679-8131
www.lightolier.com

LiteTouch, Inc.
(801) 486-8500
www.litetouch.com

Lucifer Lighting
(800) 879-9797
www.luciferlighting.com

Lutron
(610) 282-3800
www.lutron.com

Vantage Point Products
(562) 946-1718
www.vantagepointcorp.com

Mounts/Lifts

Auton Motorized Systems
(661) 257-9282
www.auton.com

Cabinetronics
(760) 738-8505

Chief Manufacturing
(800) 582-6480
www.chiefmfg.com

Concealed Entertainment
(619) 296-4330
www.concealed
entertainment.com

Inca Corp.
(310) 808-0001
www.inca-tvlifts.com

Lucasey
(800) LUCASEY
www.lucasey.com

OmniMount Systems, Inc.
(800) MOUNT IT
www.omnimount.com

Peerless
(708) 865-8870
www.peerlessindustries.com

Premier Mounts
(800) 368-9700
www.pmpi.com

SVS, Inc.
(850) 522-4747
www.svslifts.com

Vantage Point Products
(562) 946-1718
www.vantagepointcorp.com

Remote Controls

AMX
(469) 624-8000
www.amx.com

Crestron
(888) CRESTRON
www.crestron.com

Elan
(859) 269-7760
www.elanhomesystems.com

Gemini Electronics
(973) 471-9050
www.gemini-usa.com

Harman/Kardon
(800) 422-8027
www.harmankardon.com

Home Theater Master

See *Universal Remote Control*

Lexicon
(781) 280-0300
www.lexicon.com

Madrigal
(860) 346-0896
www.madrigal.com

Marantz
(800) 270-4533
www.marantz.com

Niles Audio
(305) 238-4373
www.nilesaudio.com

One for All
(925) 373-7900
www.oneforall.com

Onkyo
(800) 229-1687
www.onkyousa.com

Philips
(800) 531-0039
UK: 0870 900 9070
www.philips.com

RCA (Thomson)
(800) 336-1900
www.rca.com

Recoton
(407) 333-8900
www.recoton.com

Remote Technologies, Inc.
(RTI)
(952) 253-3100
www.rticorp.com

Sony
(800) 222-SONY
UK: 08705 1119999
www.sony.com

Universal Remote Control

Home Theater Master
(914) 835-4484
www.universal-remote.com

Xantech
(818) 362-0353
www.xantech.com

Zenith
(847) 391-7000
www.zenith.com

Seating

Acoustic Innovations
(800) 983-6233
www.acousticinnovations.com

Bass Industries
(800) 346-8575
www.bassind.com

CinemaTech Seating
(972) 381-1071
www.cinematechseating.com

Continental Seating
(972) 417-2282
www.continental.com

Fortress Seating
(800) 873-2828
www.fortresseating.com

Innovative Theaters
Irwin Seating
(905) 820-6577
www.irwinseating.com

Theatre Design Associates
(312) 829-8703
www.theatredesign.com

TK Theaters
(212) 244-2404
www.tktheaters.com

PHOTOGRAPHY CREDITS

Artcoustic/www.artcoustic.com, 20; 73

Courtesy of Atlanta Home Theater, 69; 94; 95; 96; 97; 98;
    107 (bottom); 125; 128; 130; 131

B & W Loudspeakers/www.bwspeakers.com, 75

Ballog/Steinkamp, 59; 104; 127

Courtesy of Boltz Steel Furniture/www.boltz.com, 37; 144

Courtesy of Canton Electronics Corporation/www.canton.de, 8;
    12; 47

Benny Chan/Fotoworks, 81; 82; 83

Randall Cordero, 11; 24; 31; 34; 45; 57; 63; 92; 115; 118;
    133; 134

Adam Crocker, 18; 56; 71; 106; 119; 120; 129

Carlos Domenech, 28; 41; 48; 64; 89; 105; 116

Carlos Domenech/Charles Greenwood, Design, 61

Courtesy of ddc, domus design collection/www.ddcnyc.com, 32;
    103

Allen Fine, 38; 136; 137

Sam Gray, 10 (right); 36; 51; 107 (top); 112

Steve Gross & Susan Daley/Glenn Gisler, Design, 54

Steve Gross & Susan Daley/Mary Beth DeFillipis, Design, 76

Steve Gross & Susan Daley/Joe Kremmer, Design, 78

Jackson Hill, 39; 121

Courtesy of IKEA/www.ikea.com, 5; 35; 62

Courtesy of Infinity Systems/www.harman.com, 7 (right); 23; 25;
    70

Courtesy of Innovative Theatres/www.innovativetheatres.com, 6;
    102; 111

Theo Kalomirakis, 123; 132

David Kessler, 10 (left); 14; 27; 42; 43; 52; 53; 58; 66; 85;
    86; 93; 109

John Edward Linden/Tom Carson Architects, 17

John Edward Linden/Abramson Teiger, Architects, 68

John Edward Linden/A.C. Martin & Partners, 79

Courtesy of MartinLogan/www.martinlogan.com, 9

Jay Meepos, Concepts by J, 44

Courtesy of Onkyo Corporation/www.onkyousa.com, 13; 49

Tim Street-Porter, 80 (left)

Tim Street-Porter/KAA Architects, Chris Barrett Design, Inc., 90;
    91

Courtesy of Rotel/www.rotel.com, 30

Courtesy of Sharp Electronics/www.sharpelectronics.com, 7 (left);
    15

Courtesy of SIM2/www.sim2usa.com, 22

Courtesy of Sound City, 72

Steven P. Widoff, 55

ABOUT THE AUTHOR

Krissy Rushing is the executive editor of the *Stereophile Guide to Home Theater* and *Home Theater Buyer's Guide*, former executive editor of the *Home Theater Interiors*, and former managing editor for *Home Theater* magazine and *Digital Home Entertainment*. A leading authority in audio/video interior design and technology with more than seven years industry experience, Rushing has written and edited hundreds of articles on every conceivable facet of the home-theater experience.

With an in-depth knowledge of budget, mid-level, and high-end systems, along with A/V architecture and design integration, A/V componentry, home automation, and digital technology, Rushing has been a frequent contributor to other high-tech publications including *Wired* and *Audio/Video Interiors*. She has consulted and collaborated with some of the top home theater designers in the world. Rushing is also a Kundalini yoga instructor and resides in Los Angeles, California.

ACKNOWLEDGMENTS

This book would not have been possible without the knowledge I've gained working with my friends at *Stereophile Guide to Home Theater, Home Theater, Home Theater Interiors,* and *Audio Video Interiors* for the last decade. I would also like to thank B&W, Rotel, Infinity, Sharp, Onkyo, Canton, Atlanta Home Theater, TK Theaters, MartinLogan, Innovative Theaters, IKEA, Artcoustic, Sony, Sound City, SIM2, Randy Cordero, and all the other excellent photographers for providing the gorgeous photography in this book, along with Betsy Gammons, photo editor, for coordinating all that photography. Thanks also to my editor, Mary Ann Hall, for her excellent polishing abilities and to Tank Menzies, whose support was invaluable.